# SNOW MUCH LOVE

DONNA SNOW KING

Snow Much Love
Donna Snow King
Published October 2023
Heirloom Editions
Imprint of Jan-Carol Publishing, Inc.

Illustrations: Don Grimm


ISBN: 978-1-962561-04-4
Library of Congress Control Number: 2023949246

You may contact the publisher:
Jan-Carol Publishing, Inc.
PO Box 701
Johnson City, TN 37605
publisher@jancarolpublishing.com
www.jancarolpublishing.com

*This book is dedicated to:*

*Almighty God who created me, Jesus Christ who saved me,*

*The Holy Spirit who comforts me,*

*My Mother and Daddy who taught me so many life lessons*
*I could never learn in school.*

*My brother and sister, as we learned and shared life through the years*
*and examples we taught each other.*

*I am forever grateful to God for my family.*

# Author's Note

There are those that say I have a way with words, and maybe I do, maybe I don't. You will have to be the judge. So many things I say – some call them "Donnaism's" – are from pages of my life. As I began to write them down, I was reminded of the many fun times as I grew up and all the experiences that went with it. Within the walls of this book, you will find a collection of true stories from my life. With each one I wrote down, I found myself laughing and reliving them all over again. My prayer is that, as you read them, you too will begin to remember things from your life that bring a smile to your face.

# Contents

# And look, you're still alive...

Back when all three of us kids were still at home, there were a lot of conveniences young people enjoy today that we didn't have back then. This story will showcase one of them "land lines" – no cell phones. And when I say land line, I mean the phone was attached to the wall. No special features on the phone systems, either, like call waiting or caller I.D.

There were two phones (remember land lines?) – one in the kitchen on the wall, and the other one sat in our parents' bedroom on the night stand. I was upstairs cleaning my room when I could hear the faint sound of a phone ringing. All three of us kids would run to the top of the stairs to see if one of our names might be called. It was a real treat to get a phone call back then.

As I said, I was upstairs cleaning my room, when I heard the phone ring. After a few moments, I heard Daddy holler up the stairs, "Donna, the phone's for you!"

Now, I had been keeping a secret. There was a boy at school that I really liked... and I think he liked me back. He would tease me at school and write me notes. On some of the notes, he would draw a heart. At the ripe old age of 12, I just knew we would grow up and get married. Boy howdy, was I way off!

Anyway, I go running down the stairs to see Daddy standing over by his bedroom door grinning from ear to ear. "It's a boy," he said. My heart literally jumped!

So, I ran up to the kitchen phone and took about five seconds to compose myself before I picked the phone up to say hello. Didn't want him to think I was too anxious to talk. Us girls have to play a little hard to get, you know.

So, I said hello in the most nonchalant voice I could muster at that moment, trying to hide my excitement. Well, the usual conversation took place – he said hi; I said hi; he said what are you doing; I said nothing; I asked what are you doing; he said nothing. Then we talked about school. We talked about everything we could think of… then silence.

He asked me if I liked him, to which I responded, *yes, I did.* Then I asked him if he liked me, to which he responded yes. Now, I ask you, how much better could my life get at that moment?

He said, "Well, if you like me and I like you, does that mean we are going steady?"

Now, let me stop here and explain. "Going steady" is a term that probably dates me a long, long time ago. It was a terminology we used to say we really liked each other, better than anyone else. So, that meant we were "going steady." And then you have the benefits of going steady: sitting in the school cafeteria and eating lunch together, walking from class to class while he would carry my books… oh, the bliss of going steady.

Nowadays, I hear it's called "we're talking." I will never forget the first time I heard this phraseology. I looked at them and said, "What? Of course you're talking."

So, I got schooled on the terms of modern day "going steady."

Anyway, back to my "going steady" story. The phone conversation was going well as far as I was concerned. Probably had been talking for about 8–10 minutes when all of the sudden, I got this very strange feeling, kinda like the one when you think someone is staring at you. I looked around and could not see anyone, but I couldn't shake the feeling… then, it dawned on me!

About the same time as the revelation came to me, I heard Daddy say, "Donna, do you want me to hang up the phone now?"

I was so mad, embarrassed, and shocked that even I didn't know what to say. Felt it would be best to cut the phone call short, so I said my bye and quickly hung the phone back up. Oh, my gosh, my weekend was ruined. I cried, I moped around, I was a mess. And all of this over a boy!

Daddy must have sensed I was upset and came out of their bedroom, and I might add he came out laughing. I told him how upset I was, to which he replied, "And look, you're still alive."

Needless to say, this didn't make me feel any better. The first thought was how in the world could I possibly face my new boyfriend at school... I will just die.

So, Monday rolled around and, while reluctant, off to school I went. Well, I was right; he wasn't speaking to me, and I couldn't wait to get home to tell Daddy what he had caused. He avoided me in the hallways, he avoided me in the cafeteria. So finally, I couldn't stand it anymore. I knew where his last class of the day was and walked up there, waiting for him to come out.

Now he would have no choice but to talk to me. When he came out of that classroom, there I was waiting for him. He knew that the jig was up and would have to talk to me. I started out by asking him why he was avoiding me. Was it because of my dad? He looked at me like a calf at a new gate and said, "Huh?"

Now I'm looking at him like a calf at a new gate. He said, "I thought you were mad because of my dad." To which I said, "Huh?" I shook my head and said, "Wait a minute, this conversation isn't making any sense, you go first."

He said he was so sorry, but his dad had kept telling him to get off the phone as he was expecting an important call. (Side note, there was not a "call waiting" convenience on our phones at that time either. So, when someone was trying to call you and if someone was already on the line, it would ring a busy signal.) Evidently, his dad had been telling him for quite some time to get off the phone, to which he kept ignoring. Bottom line is, his dad got fed up with him not minding him, took the phone out of his hand, and hung it up.

So, my lightning-fast mind was beginning to put two and two together, and this time I was coming up with four. I figured out that his dad taking the phone away and hanging it up happened at the exact same time that Daddy asked me if I wanted him to get off the phone. So that meant he never heard what my Daddy said, which meant I didn't have to be embarrassed any longer.

Quickly I said, "It's okay, I understand, you got in trouble with your dad." There was no way I was telling him what my dad did, no sir, not even on a bet.

After our conversation, everything was back to normal, at least for a while. He broke up with me at the end of the school year. Said summer was here and he needed to keep his options open. What? I was ready to throttle him! Heartbroken at 12 years old. Well, it did last for a whole week, then I was over him. Puppy love on steroids.

**Lesson learned:** *Always pay attention to who could be on the other end of the phone before you say something that might embarrass yourself. Or get all your facts before you draw any conclusions.*

# Corn-fed, strapping woman...

I sure hope your opinion of me doesn't change when you read the next line of my story. But I really would like to *slap* the first person who ever said, "Sticks and stones may break my bones, but names will never hurt me."

And in trying to be transparent, let's be clear here. I am not talking about a little "tap" on their cheek. Oh, no ma'am, I am talking about bringing it up from the floor, slapping them from a vertical to a horizontal position! In my estimation, it had to have been a man. That's right, you heard me – a man! Now that I got that off my chest, let's get on with the story.

Suffice it to say, I have been called a lot of names in my life – some good, some bad, and some... well, let's say really really bad. However, like Daddy said, it's not what someone calls you, it's what you answer to that matters. I have the perfect example to share with you. Just the other day, someone called me pretty. Well, if the truth be told, they said I was pretty annoying. But thinking about Daddy's advice, I chose to only pull out the positive and let the negative go down the proverbial drain.

Sometimes, friends can actually call you a "name" or insinuate something about you that is either not nice or less than flattering. That turned out to be the case with my friend, Roger. Now, Roger is, in my estimation, a gentle giant and has a heart of gold. However, on this particular day, my opinion of him was not quite so gentle. In fact, at that moment, my opinion of him didn't amount to a hill of beans.

As I recall, it was one Sunday after church, and several of us had gone out to eat. We were having such a great time together that we decided to meet up over at my house and continue "hanging out." Once everyone fixed them something to drink and found a comfortable place to sit, the subject quickly turned to relationships and what all we assumed people are looking for in a mate. Of course, it takes all kinds of people to make the world go round, so the conversation was actually very interesting. When it came time for Roger to put in his "two cents worth," that's when it happened.

Roger was describing his "perfect mate" to us. He was believing his perfect woman would be tiny and petite, just like the pastor's wife. Now, picture this: the pastor's wife was maybe 5'3", and Roger stood 6'4". I looked at him, and trying to be as delicate in my tone of voice as I could, said, "Are you sure about that? You are such a big man." To which his response was, oh, yes, he knows his future wife will be beautiful, tiny and petite... not a "corn-fed, strapping woman like you, Donna."

That is when time stood still, and I was truly at a loss for words. Can you feature that? Me, at a loss for words? I just kept staring at him, nodding my head knowingly, trying to maintain composure. Didn't dare look at anybody else in the room.

Roger just kept on going with his description of a perfect mate, and I was sitting there trying to keep from losing my temper. He just called me a "corn-fed, strapping woman!" I admit I am tall – 5'9" to be exact, and I am big-boned liked the women on my mother's side of the family, and I weigh... Well, that's not important. Should I take offense to that? Was he just trying to "get my goose?" I couldn't decide whether I should laugh or cry...

So, for the next few minutes, what seemed like hours, I sat there with a half grin on my face, keeping a close eye on him. Because if he so much as giggled or laughed, it was about to be game on. I would have jumped on him like stink on a skunk.

A few days later, I just couldn't help myself any longer. I had to know how he meant that. So, the next time I saw him, I got my nerve up, reared back, and asked him about calling me a "corn-fed, strapping woman." This was my attempt at finding out exactly how he meant it. To which he replied, "You are such a strong and beautiful woman. That is the highest compliment I could think of to say at the time." And to cap it all off, he just stood there with such a sweet smile on his face. It was at this moment when it dawned on me that he really meant it as a compliment and not an insult.

**Lesson learned:** *When someone says something to you and you're not really sure how to take it, I strongly suggest waiting a few minutes before jumping all over them. To you, it may be an insult, but to them it may have been meant as a huge compliment.*

# Dig a grave, ready for a dead man!

Until recently, I have not thought about this saying for oh, so many years. As a matter of fact, it came back to my remembrance while looking at a house that was up for auction.

Whenever there was a house up for auction, Toni and I always made sure to arrive as early as was permitted. We wanted to take our time looking the house over and not be rushed deciding as to whether to bid, and if so, how much to bid. Then, if we decided we really didn't want the house, but we could tell a competitor wanted it... Well, let's just say we had no problem running the bid up, especially if it was Randy.

As Toni and I were walking around the house, looking it over and taking measurements, I noticed two ditches at the back of the property. So, being the curious type of person I am, I meandered back there to look. That's when I turned left onto memory lane. The people, the house, the cold weather, and everything else took a back seat to my daydream.

My mind was recalling the events of a really funny day on the job a few decades earlier. The day's weather was almost perfect – not too hot and not too cold. And the job we were working on, being on the edge of town, meant there wasn't as much city noise. The lady we were working for was so sweet, offering us tea, water, and even sandwiches for lunch. Almost like the perfect job and the perfect day, or at least as close as

I had seen one be. One thing about her home that stuck out in my mind wasn't her house; it was her greenhouse in the backyard. She saw my infatuation with her greenhouse and asked me if I would like to see inside. I stood there kinda hesitant because I didn't want to get in trouble with Daddy. Then I heard Daddy say, "Go ahead, Donna, go look," so I jumped up and said, "Oh, yes, ma'am, I would love to."

Her greenhouse was so big and held some of the prettiest flowers I had ever seen. We talked so much about plants and the different flowers. She shared with me some of her little tricks for making plants grow bigger and the blooms to stay prettier longer than normal. We had a great visit.

Her greenhouse smelled as pretty as it looked. All the fragrances in that building were intoxicating. After my tour, I told the lady I had better get back to helping Daddy before he docked my paycheck.

When I came out of the greenhouse, there was a stranger there helping. I asked Daddy who this guy was. He replied that he was a young man who had walked up and asked for a handout, saying he was hungry. Now, Daddy never would turn away anyone that was hungry, so he told this man he would pay him a day's wages and feed him if he worked with us on this job. Daddy was, and still is, a very hard-working man. In other words, you don't "goof off" on the job. He expected his full day of labor, to which he was always more than fair with wages.

Now I am trying to size this guy up, and I couldn't decide if he really wanted to work or not. But Daddy always gave someone the benefit of the doubt, a trait I think we all should have. To me, he was a little bit less than enthusiastic about being given food and wages. Anyway, in trying to practice what Daddy was teaching me, I too decided to give him the benefit of the doubt.

As we were working, the rest of the crew and I were trying to make him feel at ease, so we were all talking amongst ourselves. Some of the guys got to gigging him about how he had better step up the pace if he expected the boss to keep him. The man asked, "Well, what happens if he doesn't like the work I do?"

The men replied, "Well, son, you see, it's like this... He just gets rid of them, and we never see them again. No one ever sees them again."

This guy's eyes opened up as big as saucers – you know, the whole deer in the headlights look.

I just started giggling under my breath, because I didn't want to give away the prank the crew was playing on this guy. Figured it was his "indoctrination " into the house-moving field. All newcomers get it; they did it to me, and he ain't no better.

As I turned to walk away, I could see his Adam's apple go up and down as he took a big swallow, taking all this in.

A short time later, Daddy was having to kinda get onto this guy as he was taking too many breaks. Later, Daddy told me he could tell the man was not used to manual labor.

Anyway, about thirty minutes or so later, Daddy hollered out, "Somebody dig a grave, ready for a dead man!" Which, in "house-moving" means to dig a ditch to brace off for something.

In a matter of seconds, we all heard the most awful commotion and scream. So, around the house we all ran, just in time to see the backside of this young man running across the front yard and down the road.

Daddy asked one of the guys what happened, to which they replied, "I don't know, boss. You hollered at us to dig a grave ready for a dead man, he dropped his blocks, and he started running. Poor man never got lunch or any of his wages, did he?"

Daddy walked on around the house, and I asked the guys, "Okay, what really happened?"

To which they replied when they were able to stop laughing, "When your dad called out for a grave to hold a dead man, we looked this young boy in the eyes and said, 'We tried to warn you.'"

**Lesson learned:** *Don't always believe everything you hear. When in doubt, always ask questions.*

# Do you want some of this?

Believe it or not, there was a time when you would get all dressed up to go downtown shopping. I'm talking a dress, hat, heels, and gloves. I can remember going shopping downtown with Grandma Snow, which was a huge treat for me.

Now, Grandma Snow, Daddy's mother, took her shopping seriously. Not only did she get "all dressed up," but also, anyone with her (including me) had to be dressed up, too – a frilly dress (some dresses had stiff slips under it to make my dress stand out), socks, dress shoes, and to top it all off... either a hat on my head or a bow in my hair.

As we walked up and down the isles in the department store, everyone was saying "good morning" or "good afternoon," whichever applied. And all the time, they were looking each other up and down to see if someone else looked as cute as they thought they looked. Did any of what I just said make sense?

It was almost like a contest as to who had the best matching dress, shoes, and hat. And Lord, have mercy if you saw someone wearing the same dress and hat two Saturdays in a row! Why, that was just unheard of... If you ever stopped to visit, it was always polite to tell the other women how lovely they looked and how well dressed and polite their children were. Then, if someone pointed out that the lady standing over by cosmetics was wearing the exact same dress as last Saturday, quicker than you could blink twice, someone would say, "Oh, bless her heart."

At first, I thought, *how nice... Grandma and all these ladies sure blessed a lot of hearts.* And they said it with such emphasis. Grandma told me that they were being sarcastic, but in a nice way.

In case you are trying to figure out the time period all of this was taking place, let me give you a few hints. You will find it hard to believe, but I have dialed and talked on a phone that was attached to the wall, walked a lot without counting my steps, washed dishes by hand (that's right – no dishwasher!), hung the sheets out on the clothesline to dry and loved the fragrance, and ate a meal without taking a picture of it.

Also, it was a time when there were no cell phones, meaning no evidence. Don't laugh – I know there's some of you who know what I'm talking about.

Then came "the malls," where everything was under one roof. This also created a lifestyle of hanging out at the mall all day. And if that wasn't awesome enough, they put movie theaters in the malls, and food courts! The downside to this was almost all the stores downtown started closing; a whole way of life was disappearing. No more hustle and bustle on Saturdays.

Now I have lived long enough to see an old way of life and shopping come back to downtown areas that are being revitalized. Kind of like a full circle, if you will.

The story begins with one of my second cousins on my Daddy's side named Peggy. She and her mother took her three children – the youngest being in a stroller, the two older ones being eight and ten – on a Saturday morning shopping trip downtown. Remember, this called for hats, dresses, gloves, and heels. They were always shopping, looking for dresses. According to Peggy, you just never knew when you might need a new "frock" for a special occasion. Back in this day, a frock meant a really nice dress.

The events to follow were told to me by my cousin, Peggy. Since they lived in an era when your children were raised with a firm hand, the only explanation I can offer is that there must have been a full moon somewhere. Peggy and her mother were looking at the dresses and trying to decide on which size and which color, when all of a sudden...

They heard a lot of giggling along with the pitter-patter of children's feet. As they were turning to listen in the direction of all the noise, they realized the older children were not where they were supposed to be, which means all the noise and commotion was being caused by her children.

They turned and looked just in time to see a wave of hangers going up and down, with the children underneath giggling and laughing. It appears the children had made a game of running in and out of the clothes racks. Peggy looked at her mother and asked her to take the dress and the baby, and she would meet her at the checkout counter. She had a situation to handle.

Peggy proceeded to go in the direction of the giggling and the waving of the clothes. She followed the wave of the clothing and positioned herself at the end of the rack, where her two little hoodlums would eventually come out. As they came out from under the clothes rack, both children came to an abrupt halt, almost running into their mother. Peggy laughed, telling me they were two shocked children whose young lives just passed before their eyes.

The sales lady standing there had an apparent look of disapproval on her face as she watched Peggy correct her children. Peggy looked at both of them and said, "You two know better. Your father and I didn't raise you like this!"

Peggy hadn't been so embarrassed in all her life.

Peggy and her husband's philosophy was to correct the child right there and NOT just wait till you get them home. Reaching down, Peggy took off one of her high heels, grabbed the heel part with her hand, and whipped them both with the bottom part of the shoe. Both children standing there started crying, holding their bottom. Peggy put her high heel back on and headed to the check-out counter with both children following her like the Pied Piper. As Peggy was paying for the dress, the sales lady decided to show her disapproval of how the situation was handled by grunting and clearing her throat in disappointment, clearly loud enough to get Peggy and her mother's attention.

Peggy had all she could handle and finally had to speak up to the sales lady, saying, "I perceive that you do not like the way I handled the situation with my children?"

To which the sales lady responded, "No, I did not." To which Peggy replied, "These are my children that I love dearly. I love them when they're good, and I love them enough to correct them when they misbehave. Therefore, I suggest that, unless you want some of what they just got, you had better hand me my receipt and keep your disapproval to yourself."

And here is the rest of the story.

You're probably wondering if Peggy and her mother ever went back to that store. Well, they did... and when the same sales lady saw Peggy coming, she hid in the ladies' dresses, much in the same way the children had done that day.

**Lesson learned:** *It may be in your best interest not to interfere with a mother correcting her children who have misbehaved.*

# Don't hold back; tell me how you really feel...

Several years ago, someone wrote a book about the differences between men and women, basically talking about how differently we handle situations.

I had heard about the book, and to be honest, the title intrigued me. It so happened that a friend of mine had a copy and loaned it to me to read. It was very interesting reading, and there was a lot of truth in it. Their summary was no surprise... women talk their problems out with their girlfriends, and men either go into their man-cave or put their fix-it hats on. Depending on the people involved, sometimes this can cause an unhealthy relationship. It would be like trying to mix oil and water... not a good combination. Can I get an amen?

For most of us, men or women, there always seems to be that one relationship that turns out to be more trouble than it's worth. And that is where this story begins...

A girlfriend of mine (we will call her Suzi, though it's not her real name as I want to protect the innocent) was in one of "those relationships," and one Saturday night she called me crying hysterically. And as a true friend does, I told her I was there for her and asked what was going on, what I can do to help, and if I need to bring a shovel. This was during a time of "pre-cell phones," when the phone was actually attached to a physical telephone line in the house – no caller ID, no call waiting, no call forwarding. So, as not to bore you with details, let me tell you this: if you called a number and it rang and rang and rang, this meant no one was at home, or they just weren't answering the phone. If the phone rang a busy signal, that means someone was on the phone talking and had no idea anyone was trying to call, as there wasn't a "beep" feature.

Well, she was crying so hard that she was snot-slinging and having a hard time catching her breath heaving from the tears. To hear her tell it, her world had come to an end. And like all good girlfriends do, I listened, and I listened, and I listened. So, here is her story in a nutshell...

Her boyfriend (let's call him Bob, because Bob is his real name, and I don't care anything about protecting the guilty) had been professing his never-ending love to her for several months, telling her she was his one true love, would bring her flowers to school, and even got her the most beautiful homecoming mum you have ever seen. Then, she finds out that he had also been professing his never-ending love for another girl... oops!

Of course, my first thought was, *How in the Sam Hill did he juggle two girls?* Well, guess what? They were at two different high schools.

I told her, "Let it out, let it all out. If you don't, you might explode." To which she commenced to unloading, and I mean she *unloaded.*

They were at the homecoming football game, when Suzi saw some other girl wearing a homecoming mum that looked identical to hers. You may be saying to yourself, *All homecoming football mums look the same. Why would another girl's homecoming mum even get her attention?*

In Bob's infinite wisdom, he put his jersey number on one of the streamers, on both mums! And this was the beginning of the end for Bob.

Bob's downfall began with both Suzi and this other girl running into each other in the bathroom. They were saying how beautiful each other's mum looked, and how strangely they looked alike, right down to the streamer with their boyfriend's jersey number on it. What are the odds, right? Evidently, they both realized at the same time that there was a rat in the wood pile somewhere. This was not adding up. After exchanging information, they both felt the need to go find Bob and give him a piece of their mind.

When they found him, he was hanging out with some of his friends, who must have known what Bob had done, because when they saw both girls standing side by side behind Bob, well, you might describe the look on their faces as if they'd just seen a ghost.

When Bob turned around, there stood both of his "girlfriends," both wearing the mums he had gotten for them. So, Suzi commenced in on Bob first, hollering, "After all the things you told me... 'I love you, you're the best girlfriend a boy could have.' I thought you meant it when you said you loved me, and now I see you have another girlfriend!"

Well, she had drawn a crowd to watch the takedown, as it seems several people had heard about what was going on. Like they say, good gossip travels fast. It appeared there was more action going on in the parking lot than the football field.

Bob got flustered and probably embarrassed looking around at the crowd that was gathering and wanted desperately to lash back out at her. And he did. Open mouth, insert foot. That's when it all went south...

Bob let his anger take over and blurted out that they weren't the only two girlfriends he had; he had another one, and he named her and her high school. Oh, my gosh! As soon as he finished his screaming speech, he quickly realized what he had just done and stood there like the cat that ate the canary.

Of all the football games to miss, why did I have to miss this homecoming? This "show" would have definitely been worth the price of admission.

So, my friend and the other girl just looked at each other, as if forming an alliance, and turned to look at Bob. They were about to commence in on him – chew him up and spit him out! And I bet you Bob's life flashed before his eyes. They must have turned loose on him big time.

Suzi told me what she said to Bob: "I told him he was the meanest, ugliest, worst-kissing, two-timing, pond scum, slithering snake, yellow-bellied idiot I had ever met in my life!" To which I replied, "Don't hold back; tell me how you really feel." Ha!

You may be wondering how in the world he got caught. Turns out, his sneaky plan had a big hole in it. When you buy a girl a homecoming mum, you are expected to go with her to their homecoming football game. Well, what happens when those two schools end up playing each other at homecoming? Yep, you guessed right... one of Bob's other girlfriends was from the opposing school's football team at our homecoming.

So, Bob had a very big problem on his hands – how to take two different girls to the same homecoming game. It was our homecoming game, Haltom High School, and our archrivals, Richland High School. Poor Bob! Turns out, after getting everything off her chest, my friend Suzi was okay. She didn't need the shovel after all.

**Lesson learned:** *Don't be like Bob! And if you ever have a girlfriend that needs to vent, be there for her and tell her, "Don't hold back; tell me how you really feel!" Then, be prepared for the flood gates to open.*

# Don't make me pray for you...

This story is completely from a child's perspective, probably around the age of 9–10. So, try not to judge me too harshly. While I did grow up holding onto the values taught to me as a child, I have learned to handle similar situations a little bit differently.

To help you understand this "saying," I felt it best to give you a little background on my family. Growing up, my mother was raised Baptist, and my Daddy was raised Methodist. When they married, they decided their marriage would be stronger if they kept God at the center of their world, which led them to promising each other to stay in church. When they started "their family," they would be raised in the church, too. True to their promise to each other, when we came along, guess who went to church every Sunday? We did.

All three of us were raised in a Southern Baptist church here in Fort Worth, Texas. Of course, just like any kid, there were many times none of us wanted to get up early on Sunday morning; we wanted to sleep in. Looking back, I am glad they dragged us to church. They saw to our educational upbringing as well as our spiritual. For that, I will be forever grateful. Some of the things they taught us were faith, respect, helping others, and finally, praying before every meal.

One time, when we went out to eat, I asked Daddy, "Why did we have to pray over everything we ate?"

He looked at me and asked, "Did you see the cook actually cook the food?"

"No, sir, I didn't... Oh, I get it."

Daddy said, "Well, that's one reason we pray. However, the main reason is to thank God that we have food to eat."

Let me set up the events that led to my "situation" that day.

I was so young that I actually don't remember my Sunday school teacher's name. Now that I think about it, on the off chance she reads this book, she will probably be glad I forgot her name.

Is it just me, or does it seem like kids get crueler to each other as the years go by? Back in my day, kids either made fun of you to your face, giggled with their friends behind your back as you walked by, or passed notes around about you. Today, bullying has reached a whole new level, especially when you factor in cyber-bullying.

You may say, *Donna, you are nuttier than a fruit cake. All kids, all through the years, are the same.* To which I would say, did you hit your head? Kids back in my day had more respect for others and their property than most kids today. I see news reports on TV every day involving kids who have committed crimes, something that didn't happen very often when I was growing up. Although, I will admit there are still some moms who won't stand for the bad behavior.

On the news one night, they were showing live coverage involving several kids causing trouble and destroying property. One of the boys involved had no clue that his mother was within 100 miles of him. Well, guess what? As it turned out, she was.

And even though he was wearing a ski mask, trying to hide his identity, his mother recognized him. Children cannot hide the way they walk, their mannerisms, or voice from their parents – especially moms.

She went running up to him, grabbed the ski mask and pulled it off, then grabbed him by the hair on his head and went to dragging him and giving him a good chewing out. She busted his butt with her purse, all at the same time. This woman was talented, for sure. I found myself hollering, "You go, mom, handle your business!"

Back when I was growing up, I highly respected my parents, knowing how far to "push" things. And I *knew* where the line was. I think this young man just found his "line." With that being said, that is where my story really starts.

Growing up, I was – let's say – a string bean. No shape whatsoever. While all the girls around me were starting to "fill out," Donna wasn't. I was really starting to think something was wrong with me. If we are honest, I believe we have all thought this.

So, one fine Sunday morning as Mother and Daddy took us all to church, all of the previous weeks' hurts and insults were stirring around in my mind. I was actually practicing the hurt over and over in my mind. (For the record, this is never a good thing to do.) As it turned out, the lesson for that Sunday in our class was about praying for your enemy.

Our teacher started out the class with the first part of that scripture that tells us to pray for our enemies. If they are hungry, we are to feed them; if they are thirsty, give them something to drink. Well, needless to say, all of my Sunday school classmates could not believe it.

"What?" we all said at the same time. "If anyone is mean to me, I'm gonna be mean right back to them."

Our teacher had a very overwhelming look of shock on her face. She quickly got our attention and said we should listen to the rest of the scripture and story, telling us we need to get all the facts before we make a rash decision. Remember, there are always three sides to a story, she told us. There's your side, their side, and in the middle lies the truth. Everyone tends to have a slanted opinion, always in their favor.

We all looked around at each other, and quickly realized she was right. So, we calmed down and decided to hear the rest of the story, sitting on the edge of our seats waiting for her answer.

In the Bible, there is scripture that says we are to pray for our enemy and anyone that does mean things to us. For most of us, when someone does something mean to us, we want revenge. Most often, we turn around to be mean to them. However, the Bible tells us that revenge belongs to the Lord...

But there is more to the story. For by doing this, you will heap burning coals of fire on their heads.

We all sat back in our chairs, trying to wrap our young minds around what we had just learned. Jerry sat back in his chair, crossed his arms, and said, "Now that's more like it."

Not really sure, but I think our Sunday school teacher was a little skeptical that we had gotten the true meaning of our lesson that morning. And I can say from personal experience, she would be correct.

Fast forward to the next day, Monday morning. I literally couldn't wait to get to school!

Walking down the hallways, my radar was on high alert just waiting for someone to be mean to me, because I knew how to deal with them. Now, I wasn't gonna waste my ammo on just any insult; it would have to be a deserving one.

Well, it didn't take too long, and here it came:

"Oh, look, here comes Donna. You look like a thin fence rail. Are you a girl or a boy?"

Now, in my book, I felt like that qualified as a huge insult worthy of my ammo. So, I turned around, called them out by name, walked towards them, and said, "Don't make me pray for you, 'cause if you ever say anything mean to me again, I will pray for you. And if I pray for you, God will put burning coals on your head. And when he does, your hair will burn up!"

The end result was this girl started crying and saying, "I don't want my hair to burn up!"

We were all sent to the principal's office.

**Lesson learned:** *Listen to the whole story and get all the information before you react.*

# Don't tell me why, just leave...

I would have given almost anything to have a cell phone to record the following. It would have definitely gone viral on social media.

Toni had just started "dating." Keep in mind that she is the youngest of us three kids. She got the same talk that I had gotten when I started dating:

"You had better be home by your curfew, say goodnight, and get in the house. There will be no dilly-dallying in the driveway."

Toni had started dating a young boy by the name of Tyler (not his real name). Well, the date was over, and here they come pulling in the driveway. Evidently, Toni's idea of how long it takes to say goodnight and Daddy's idea was, well, let's say two different numbers.

But in Toni's defense, let's all remember what it was like when we first started dating and going steady with the same boy. Time didn't exist, and there was always so much to talk about. There was a lot of important information to discuss, like favorite colors, birthdays, favorite songs and bands. Like I said, very important information.

Daddy was getting more agitated by the minute, pacing the floor. I was sitting there waiting for him to blow, and yes, I was enjoying every minute of it. I had already paid my dues in the whole dating thing. Now it was Toni's turn.

Something just came to me – what kind of talk did he have with Gary on the subject of dating?

I guess Gary didn't want to miss out on an opportunity to "help point out to Daddy" that Toni was breaking the rules. Or, now that I think about it, maybe he was trying to step in and help Toni... *hmmmm.*

Anyway, Gary steps up to Daddy and tells him, "Don't worry about this. I'll handle it for you."

Now, this brings up another question: why did Gary step in, and why did Daddy let him? I guess I need to ask them.

Before Daddy could really say anything, Gary was out the back door and headed toward Tyler's car.

The only thing that would have made this "action-packed movie" better would have been popcorn – oh, yes, movie-buttered popcorn!

Our driveway, being a long one, came right up beside several windows in the den, where we were watching TV. So, it was very clear that Toni's new boyfriend had pulled in the driveway and right up by the windows. At this point, I am running to the windows to listen. I was not about to miss the fireworks that I knew were coming!

Tyler and Toni had no idea that anybody was within a hundred miles. Gary walked up to the driver's side of the door and tapped on the window. When Tyler looked around, Gary gave him the hand signal to roll the window down. Evidently, Gary had startled both of them.

Tyler quickly rolled the window down, and Gary leaned in and said, "Don't tell me why, just leave."

And, yes, World War 3 was on! Toni bailed out of the passenger's side of the car, literally at the speed of sound, hot on Gary's trail. Gary is no fool; he had to have known that this wasn't going to sit well with his baby sister.

Toni chased him around the car and into the house. Tyler was in a panic trying to start his car so he could get out of the driveway.

The race was on with Toni hot on Gary's heels, through the den and up the stairs, screaming and hollering at him the whole time. Gary could hardly run from laughing so hard. I guess Daddy figured that if he wanted his son to live to see the next sunrise, he had better step in.

Daddy took control of the situation and got Toni to calm down. I think Toni didn't get in as much trouble as she would have because Gary had really embarrassed her in front of her boyfriend.

Now, in Tyler's defense, he and Toni dated for quite a while after that. He really was a nice boy. But I can tell you this – all through the rest of their time dating, they were never late, nor did they "dilly-dally" in the driveway when he brought her home from a date.

FYI... Gary and Toni may give a different spin on this story, but this is what I saw. Yep, this is my story, and I'm sticking to it.

**Lesson learned:** *Follow the rules, or take a chance on getting embarrassed.*

# Don't worry; once they get you in the light, they'll turn you loose...

You may find this hard to believe, but there were a few things I was afraid of growing up. This story is about one of them that I will openly admit to – being afraid of the dark.

It was late on a Sunday night, and we were heading home from the farm visiting Grandma and Papaw Gandee. All five of us – Daddy, Mother, Gary, Toni, and I – had a fun but long weekend, and everyone was tired. All the way home, I was thinking about all the homework I still had left to do, no getting around it. Didn't want the teacher to give me a zero, and that would have been my fate if this homework wasn't turned in on time bright and early in my first period class on Monday morning.

So, when we pulled into the driveway, all I could think about was getting out of the backseat of the car, finishing up the homework I didn't get done while at Grandma's house, getting ready for bed, and dreading school on Monday morning. My gosh, there was so much left to do before I could go to bed.

While all of us were very tired, Mother and Daddy weren't all "whiny" like us kids were. I was whiny, Gary was even whinier, and Toni was the whiniest of all. Sounds almost like that girl and the three bears, doesn't it?

When we pulled in the driveway, it was late, which meant it was dark outside. Not a single one of us in the car thought anything about it being dark. Why, you ask? Because Daddy was there. With him there, no one even thought about being scared of anything. Just his presence set us all at ease.

We got out of the car and all but staggered to the back door. As usual, Daddy made sure we were all in the house, with him being the last one in. Just like clockwork, Daddy went into his "routine" of ending his day and securing his family and house for the night. He began by making sure the door was locked, checking if the back porch light was on, making sure it's turned off, locking the back door, and closing the drapes over the sliding glass door. Once his "Daddy duties" were done, he too was ready to hit the hay (go to bed).

Just as I was dragging myself to my room, it dawned on me: *where are my schoolbooks? Where are my papers?* That's when panic mode set in.

Frantically, I turned around to Daddy and said, "Wait! Don't lock the door! I left my homework in the car."

So, Daddy pulled the drapes back, unlocked the door, reached up to turn the back porch light on, and after a small flash, the bulb went out. It was flipping dark out there! I looked at Daddy and said, "Now what am I going to do?"

He said, "Donna, you know the back porch. You know the driveway. Go on out there and get your homework."

I said, "Daddy, I can't go out there in the dark. Somebody might get me."

To which Daddy stopped, turned around, looked at me, and said, "Don't worry; once they get you in the light, they'll turn you loose."

Obviously, I didn't think that was too funny at the time. But as an adult telling this story, it is funny.

**Lesson learned:** *On the off chance that you are afraid of the dark, before you get out of the car, check the backseat and floorboards.*

# Gather my family once a year...

This isn't so much a saying as it should be a way of life.

My Great Grandpa Thoma was a mountain of a man in my eyes. There were a few things in life that he considered precious – his work ethic, name, keeping his word, providing for his family, and helping his neighbor. But at the head of his list was family.

A man of German descent, he had so much knowledge inside of him that had been passed down generation to generation. Working with his hands and building things was his specialty. He could see a problem, ponder on it, and come up with a resolution. It was his intention to see this tradition carried on, so he passed it down to his children, grandchildren, and anyone else who wanted to learn.

My Daddy was no exception; he loved his Grandpa and hung onto every word the man said, spending as much time with him as he could. From building things, growing things, hunting, and fishing, it seemed as if there wasn't anything Grandpa Thoma couldn't do.

Daddy used to tell me his Grandpa Thoma could build anything out of literally nothing. I see so much my Great Grandpa Thoma in my Daddy.

While I was very young when he graduated to Heaven, I still have memories of this man, and the picture in my mind is still as vivid as an actual photograph. Large in stature, big ole thick mustache, and a husky voice. Like I said earlier, a mountain of a man.

Great Grandpa Thoma was also known for his "stink bait" recipe. While I absolutely could not stand being around when he was making it, the bounty it reaped on the trot lines was some of the best catfish you ever tasted. And that, my friend, is a story in itself. For me, there was a complete feeling of security and wellbeing just being around him.

I can remember back to annual family reunions. The kind where everyone came to a campground, bringing food, games, and photo albums. All meals were like a huge buffet where everyone put their food out on the campsite table, and we all shared with each other. That is, of course, after we said a prayer. Daddy and all the men folk, along with some of us kids, would catch fish for the "fish fry," which was the highlight of the weekend. Grandpa Thoma's stink bait never let us down. Then, to top the meal off was all the fabulous homemade desserts and s'mores around the campfire.

As a rule, we would go to parks on a river or a lake, since just about everyone had a camper or a tent. This year, Daddy offered to host the annual reunion at our lake house up on Eagle Mountain Lake.

It really was a great place. I remember Daddy and Mother taking us out there and showing it to us when they decided to buy it. It was about two acres sitting at the end of a road. The land went right down to the river that fed into the lake. While it was awesome for fishing, Daddy never would let us swim there. Bummer!

In the beginning, we stayed in a homemade camper when we went there on the weekends, but then Daddy moved in a house that we fixed up. All the conveniences of home – bedrooms, living room, kitchen, and bathrooms. There was one modern convenience not allowed on the property: a telephone.

Daddy said this was a place for him to get away from all the hustle and bustle of work. Can't say I blamed him one little bit, because after working all day, he would come home, take a shower, and try to eat supper and watch some of his favorite shows on TV. But, as a rule, each intended "relaxing" evening was met with the phone, there at home, ringing literally up until 10:00 p.m. every night. It became a joke that he never got to see a whole show on TV or eat a hot meal, because 99 percent of the time, when the phone rang, it was a business call for him.

This was eye opening to us kids, as we never realized Daddy needed a break too. We started seeing why it was important to unplug.

The year Mother and Daddy offered to host the annual family reunion at our lake place, we were so excited. It wasn't nothing fancy, but we did have a big cement slab covered by a tin roof, the house, indoor plumbing, running water, and plenty of room for everyone to park.

Now, this is a good example of what I was describing earlier when I said my Daddy learned a lot from his Grandpa Thoma – how to take nothing and make something, knowing there was gonna be lots of kids there who would be looking forward to going swimming. A reasonable assumption, I think; you go to a lake for a family get-together, and you expect to go swimming.

So, Daddy, in his infinite wisdom, took several big cross timbers from the office with two huge, thick pieces of new plastic. After a couple of hours of work, we had a homemade swimming pool! Like I said, Daddy inherited a lot of his "can-do attitude" from his Grandpa Thoma. While we may not have had a lot of earthly possessions, we still always managed to have fun. More importantly, we had each other.

Nowadays, we have social media to stay up on friends and family outings and whatever else is going on in their lives. Pictures from the time we are born to the time Jesus calls us home to Heaven. People can even post an "in a relationship" button, which tells who they are dating, engaged to, getting married to, or even breaking up with. While I agree social media is good, it's only good in its place. That is what brings me to the heart of my story.

Grandma Snow and her sisters – Patsy Ruth, Virginia, and Mamie – were all sitting at a baby shower for one of my cousins. Oh, my gosh, I had a "buttload of cousins." (Yes, "buttload" is a real word in the dictionary. Go look it up.)

So, suffice it to say, I attended many, many wedding and baby showers. Anyway, I had reached the age where I loved to hear all the "old stories" from years gone by. My Grandma and Great Aunt's conversation was about their "Poppa" – that is what they called him. On his deathbed, he called his "girls" in to talk to them. He looked at each one of them, sharing his favorite story of them growing up and how they each carried such a special place in his heart, as well as their mother's, my Great Grandma Thoma who passed away when I was very young.

After he finished talking to each daughter, he said, "I have something I need you to promise me." Each girl promised their poppa that they would do whatever he asked.

Grandma Snow told me it was at this moment that she realized her poppa was about to go to Heaven and be with their mother.

Grandpa Thoma said, "Please gather my family once a year. That is all I ask of you." He went on to say, "I believe in my heart this will keep our family together."

And he was right. My Grandma Snow and her sisters and brothers kept their promise to their poppa. His family, even as it continued to grow, did stay together. As the years went by, we would have a family reunion. I grew up knowing my aunts and uncles, my great aunts and great uncles, my cousins, my second cousins, and even some third cousins.

However, once the "sisters and brothers" started passing away, so did the family reunions. Oh, we held on until the last Thoma daughter and son were gone. But sadly, the family reunions became few and far in between. We still "got together," as we say, once in a blue moon, but that is not near enough time spent with family. Lately, I see some of my "older" family members that I remember growing up around posting on social media about more family members I have never even met. Kinda makes me sad.

I encourage everyone, no matter the size of your family, to live by the words of my Great Grandpa Thoma who said, "Gather my family once a year, and gather your family once a year."

**Lesson learned:** *Progress is good. However, when it comes to family, keep the old-fashioned ways, and gather your family once a year.*

# Get in, sit down, shut up, and hold on...

Has anyone ever heard of a back-seat driver?

Why, of course, we all have... but what if you had a warning sign for them?

Now, I am not saying that Mother was a front-seat driver, but I will admit she would point out on occasion when Daddy wasn't driving to her liking.

Growing up, this became somewhat of a tennis match, if you will, with us kids in the backseat watching this unfold. Let me give you an example of what I am talking about.

We would all be in the car, and as usual, Daddy was driving. As we would approach a light that was clearly red, Daddy would start slowing down, but I guess he didn't slow down soon enough. Mother was quick to say, "Harold Don, Harold Don, that is a red light. Slow down."

Daddy would respond by saying, "Sweetheart, I can see the light is red, and I did start slowing down."

Another quick example... Daddy would be coming up on a stop sign with intentions to turn right. Obviously, Mother didn't think he was turning on his turn signal as soon as he should, and she felt the need to point it out. Like I said earlier, to us kids sitting in the back seat, it was just like a tennis match. Sometimes it got downright comical. It was easy to tell when their patience was running thin with each other; their "cute names" for each other were used more often and in a slightly louder and tenser voice.

Now, picture this. Daddy is what I would call a man's man, large and in charge. But being the good husband he is, he had to "rein those feelings in" when it came to Mother and his driving.

As a side note, I found out that growing up, Daddy got a lot of the same "helpful instructions" from his mother as he was learning to drive, too. When I found that out, a lot of his reactions started making sense.

Anyway, back to my original story.

Daddy took a 1973 Bluebird school bus and turned it into a camping rig. This would be the second bus he had converted. He literally lifted the hull of this bus up, pulled everything out, and started his project. By the end of the project, he had a Mack Scania engine, Allison transmission, aluminum water tanks, custom cabinets, air conditioning/heat, and bathroom with a shower – all the comforts of home under the shell of this bus.

Our bathroom on this bus was so homemade that the door was literally a piece of plywood, with the lock on the door being a rubber band. You can laugh, but it worked. Over the years, Daddy would write little funnies on the backside of the door. When using "the facility," you had a comic book to read. When asked why there was a rubber band holding the door shut, he would jokingly say "to ease any stress on the door should there be any gas in the area." He always had a smart or funny answer for everything.

Daddy did his best to take us on a vacation every summer for about one to two weeks, depending on finances. When we would stop for fuel, Daddy would look in the "phone book" for local House Movers. If he found one, he called them up, introduced himself, and asked if they had a job going. We could stop by and visit. He did this in every state we traveled across. Oh, how he loved exchanging ideas as well as "tricks of the trade" with other movers.

Daddy told me he enjoyed talking "house-moving" with other movers in these different states because he learned so much. But even more than that, he loved making new friends. By the end of the visit, this stranger became a lifelong friend. I can remember him telling me that the greatest treasure you can have in this world is that of a true friend. At first, it didn't make sense to me, but as I grew older and entered the "adult world," it came to make a lot of sense.

I remember the first summer the bus was ready to go. Everything was finished, with the exception of painting the outside. So, off we went on our family vacation in a "yellow school bus." I really think I may need therapy after running around on vacation in a yellow school bus.

This year, we were going to Disneyworld in Florida. Well, when we pulled onto the Disneyworld property, the magnitude of this place became a reality. It wasn't just big; it was gargantuan on steroids! And with a big place comes a lot of walking. As we pulled into the parking lot, a man motioned for my Daddy to get out of the long line we were in that was moving at the pace of snail and pointed us over to another lane.

At first, it was a little confusing until we realized this man was directing us to park where all the school buses parked. (Remember, our bus was still the original school bus colors – yellow with a black stripe.) So, as Daddy pulled up beside the man, he opened his side window, and told him, "Sir, this is a school bus that I converted into a camper. It's not been painted yet."

The man looked at Daddy and just smiled, telling him, "That's okay, no worries. This will get you and your family in faster. Have a blessed day here at Disneyworld." And trust me, we did.

After that vacation, Daddy said it was time to paint it, and guess what color it was? If you guessed orange, *ding, ding, ding*, you win! He painted it his favorite color, orange. Then, he went one step further and put an old brass school bell on the front above the windshields and ran a cord through the driver's side window. Every chance he got, he was ringing that school bell. People loved it.

Several years later, Daddy did something that all good sons should do. He included his mother on a vacation, but this time he was going to Alaska.

I remember the sign he painted to put on the back of the camper: "Texans going to check out the size of Alaska." On the bottom, it said, "Alaska or bust."

People really got a kick out of his signs. So, now, he not only had his wife helping him to drive, but also, he had his mother! I will not expound on that experience of driving from Texas to Alaska and back. I believe I will let your imagination do the rest.

I bet you think I forgot where I was supposed to be going, didn't you?

Now, I am down to where the saying came from...

Daddy had a friend who gave him a sticker, and guess where he put the sticker? Whenever you opened the door of the bus, he put the sticker on the steps going inside. The sticker said, "Get in, sit down, shut up, and hold on."

I am not saying that sticker was meant for anyone in particular. However, if the shoe fits...

**Lesson learned:** *If you're gonna go anywhere with H.D. Snow, I strongly suggest you not tell him how to drive.*

# Gonna have to lick that calf over...

To tell you about this saying takes me back to a time spent with someone I hold so dear to my heart: my Grandma Gandee.

If you grew up going to family gatherings such as Easter, birthdays, Thanksgiving or Christmas, you know what I mean. For my family, about 99% of all these gatherings were held at my grandparents' house. Even the 45-minute drive was exciting, knowing when the engine turned off, we were there. From where we lived in town compared to where they lived out in the country, it was truly like two different worlds. Back then, even the air seemed fresher, things moved slower, life felt more relaxing, and there wasn't so much *hurry, hurry, hurry*.

Grandma and Papaw Gandee lived out in the country about 10 miles out of town on a working farm. They raised cattle, planted, and worked the fields for hay. They worked an over-two-acre garden that yielded some of the best tasting vegetables I have ever put in my mouth. They raised bottle calves, chickens, had dairy cattle that was milked every morning and every night. They even had pigs and, yes, they stunk to high heaven!

So many memories of my weekends, summers, and family gatherings were there on their farm. It just dawned on me that neither one of them ever raised their voice to me that I can remember. No scoldings, no time outs, no leg whippings.

I have got to tell you a little funny Grandma told me. She was so embarrassed because she had so much trouble getting her kids to drink milk from the grocery store. I asked why her kids didn't like milk.

"Oh, they like milk," she said, "they just didn't like 'processed milk' from the grocery store."

Since they had grown up drinking fresh milk from the dairy barn, the store-bought milk wasn't "sweet" enough. Well, I have no opinion on the subject, as the only time I purposely drink milk is when I'm having cereal. Now, my sister, Toni… she loves milk.

One morning, Grandma was heading out the backdoor to go feed, and there standing at the edge of her backyard was a guinea. She had no idea where she came from but figured she would be gone by the next day. She wasn't.

Any animal that hung around Grandma's farm long enough got a name, and this guinea was given the name Suzi. That guinea would roost in the big oak tree, and if anyone came in that driveway… Oh, man, she let you know about it. And that is how she earned the name "Suzi, the watch guinea." All of us grandkids learned to walk a big circle around Suzi; she could be scary. She never bothered Grandma, I figured, because she fed her every day.

Grandma's farm taught me a lot of things about life. One of the lessons is that of life and death. Like baby calves being born. Seeing new life is an experience I will never forget as long as I live. Watching that momma cow give birth, then to see her start licking the baby clean.

Grandma explained to me what was happening, and then she said, "Let's go back to the house. This momma has got it from here. She will be busy licking her calf over for a while."

That was the first time I had ever heard the phrase, "licking the calf over." So, I took it she meant to clean the baby calf up.

Grandma's kitchen was originally a screened-in back porch that was eventually enclosed to be the kitchen area. On one end was a short wall of white cabinets and double porcelain sinks. She made the curtains herself – red and white checks. Her kitchen table was the old '50s look, the red and gray metal. In fact, come to think of it, she did buy them back in the '50s. She loved red.

About midways of the room was her stove, which reeked of propane, and the other end of the room was her washer and dryer with her mother's china hutch. Grandma didn't keep the usual "china" like we think of today. No, it held large serving platters that had such pretty flower patterns on them to hold family-size portions at special occasions.

At our family gatherings, all the adults got to sit at the table in the kitchen, and all of us kids sat, yep, you guessed it, at the "kids table." Now, the kids table was card tables Grandma had which usually was set up in the living room. After everyone filled their bellies, it was time to do the dishes.

Now, you may think I am crazy, but I loved doing the dishes with Grandma. We would talk and laugh. In the beginning, she told me that this was the best way to get my fingernails clean. She was right! Makes me think about the time my Daddy asked me if I wanted to go pearl diving.

"Well, of course I do, Daddy."

"Good," he said, "let's go."

And he led me straight into the kitchen and up to the sink full of dirty dishes. I was like, "Huh? Where's the pearls we are diving for?"

And he responded, "You have to look for them under the suds."

That was when I caught on – he was wanting me to wash the dishes. Through the years, I have heard it referred to as "diving for pearls," cleaning my fingernails, or busting suds.

Anyway, on my first go-around of washing dishes, I was on the right washing, and Grandma was on the left rinsing and putting them on the dish strainer to dry. Did you notice I didn't say anything about a dishwasher? Yes, this was that long ago.

So, the dishwashing was underway, and we were talking and laughing, then Grandma said, "Oops, you're gonna have to lick this calf over."

I looked at her and said, "Ma'am, what are you talking about?"

To which she responded, "Remember what we saw yesterday out in the pasture?"

Then it hit me; she meant the plate wasn't clean. She handed it back to me and, sure enough, there was a spot I missed. We both busted out laughing.

Papaw Gandee came into the kitchen to see what all the hysterical commotion was about. We were still laughing so hard that neither one of us could hardly talk. I managed to get out, "Gotta lick this calf over."

He looked at us, scratched his head, and as he turned to walk out of the room, he murmured, "Don't guess I'll ever understand women folk."

So, from that day forward, any time a job was not done right or incomplete, we always would say to each other, "Oops, you better lick that calf over again."

At this very moment as I am sitting here writing, I am laughing through some tears. Such fun times and wonderful memories. I miss her so much.

I saw a post on social media the other day that said, "What this world needs are more days shelling peas with Grandma." I agree.

**Lesson learned:** *Do it right the first time, or be prepared to do it again and again and again until you do.*

# Hide and watch.
# I'm about to take the trash out...

Let's get one thing straight before I tell you this story: if I want Daddy to know about this, I will tell him. And since the odds of him reading this are slim to none, I feel pretty safe sharing it.

As the daughter of a house-mover, and a house-mover in the making, I grew up learning how to do a lot of non-gender friendly jobs. My skill sets regarding the outside of the house ended up bigger than my skill sets regarding the inside of the house.

I graduated high school when I was 17 years old, so I went from working on the weekends and during the summer with Daddy to a full-time, tax paying employee. As the end of my senior year of high school grew near, just like every other graduating senior, I was often asked what I wanted to do with my life.

My answer then is the same answer I have today: I want to be a house-mover just like my Daddy. Now, there are those who say I am H.D. Snow made over, but in a female body. Sometimes I agree with that, and sometimes I don't. Obviously, I have always strived very hard to make my Daddy proud of me, so let me set the story up for you.

Mother and Daddy were going on a trip to Alaska in their camper. Being the oldest, I was left in charge of Gary and Toni, who were still in school at the time, and the family business. We were working on a job in Hillsboro, which is south of Fort Worth. Daddy left me his "W on H" (Work on Hand), so all the work was lined out. All I had to do was follow his instructions. The house that we were sitting down in Hillsboro was large, and we had moved it in two pieces. We didn't have skid steers or our F550 (little boom truck) at the time, so the handling of all the beams was done with the big winch truck. This made things a lot slower than they are today.

From an early age, Daddy taught me how to drive the big pull trucks. But that was strictly around on the jobsites in the beginning. His reasoning was that if I was driving the truck and working the winch line, that would put another able-bodied man on the ground to carry cribbing blocks.

On that first day, we made a lot of progress sitting the two pieces down on the new foundation, and we were feeling pretty good about ourselves. I had been bugging Charlie (not his real name) to let me drive the big winch truck back to the yard.

I said, "Okay, look, we have had a great day, and we are not carrying any beams home, so, can I please, please, please... ah, Charlie, come on, let me drive!"

He reminded me that I didn't have my CDL license.

Instant reflex on my part... I put my hands on my hips and said, "So!?"

Charlie spouted back at me, "What if your dad finds out?"

I quickly responded with, "He will only find out if you tell him, 'cause I ain't saying a word."

Truth be told, I must have worn him down, because he finally gave in and agreed to let me drive. We left the job and began making our way up the highway, and just like the song says, we were north bound and down.

Let me tell you about the truck I was driving... I love this truck so much. It is a bright, candy-apple red 1964 Mack Thermodyne, B Model. This truck has 4 sticks in it – a main with 5 gears, behind that an auxiliary with 4 gears, and behind that a brown lipe with another 4 gears. Then you had your winch line.

Probably about now, you're thinking, *man, that's a lot of gears*, and yes, it is. Daddy and Pop taught me how to put the main gear down in "Grannie" (also referred to as compound). Then you use the auxiliary and brown lipe swapping gears, and that is what is called "snorting around."

This was actually the very first winch truck that Daddy had ever ordered brand new from the factory. He went to the local Mack house and placed his order. A few weeks later he received a phone call from the Mack salesman to come in; they needed to talk. Daddy stopped by there on the way in from a job the next day. The salesman told him that the engineers in Allentown, Pennsylvania, where the trucks are built, said the truck he ordered would be "gear bound" and "wouldn't untrack."

Daddy just grinned and said, "Build the truck exactly the way I ordered it."

The salesman answered him back, "Yes, sir, will do."

And guess what? Daddy was right!

Where was I… Oh, that's right. I was north bound and down, heading back to our "yard."

I was cruising down the highway at about 60 miles per hour, which was top speed for this truck, with the windows down and no AC. Daddy said he designed this truck to pull and not to be a race truck. Daddy would joke around with people that this truck was built so strong that he could back up to the corner of "Hades," lift it up, and put a block under it. Since Daddy wasn't a cussing man, this was about as close as he got.

Oh, yeah, by the way, Daddy names all his trucks. Through the years, he had "Tarzan," "Mortgage Lifter," "Big Momma," "Spooky," "Jelly Bean," "Top Dog," "Bad Dog," "Dude," "Ruff N Ready," "Mack Daddy," and "Thelma." And this truck's name was "Big Bad John." Depending on how old you are, you may actually know where he got the name from.

Everything was going very smoothly. I could tell Charlie was relaxing, because his knuckles were no longer white from gripping the arm rest. We were cruising along, and I was minding my own business in the right lane, when we heard a bunch of honking and screaming. Charlie and I looked at each other trying to figure out where in the cornbread dickens all that noise was coming from. I looked in my side mirror, Charlie was looking in his side mirror, and we both saw them at about the same time.

It was a car full of young boys, weaving from the right side of the road to the left side of the road... back and forth, back and forth. Then, they pulled up beside me on the driver's side, looked up at the window, and seemed to be surprised when they saw a female driving. They waved at me, so I did the appropriate, cordial thing and waved back, thinking that would be the end of it.

However, I was wrong. They went to messin' with me. They would pull up and get over in front of me and start slowing down, to which I would have to respond quickly by down shifting. You have to realize, this is a big, heavy winch truck. You just don't stop these things on a dime. Then, they would pull back over into their own lane and slow down to be even with the driver's window again.

It became increasingly clear these boys were on the 9th floor of a 7-story building. In other words, they were drunk or high... not sure which.

As you can imagine, Charlie was starting to panic... and for a good reason. He could tell I was getting mad. Then came their next trick, pulling over like they were going to hit me from the side and then quickly pulling away.

I told Charlie, "These boys' elevators don't go all the way to the top!"

Charlie started yelling at me, "Donna just ignore them, just ignore them!"

I told Charlie I was trying, but it just wasn't working. I had tried ignoring them for as long as I could, and that was the longest thirty seconds of my life. When they realized that no matter how hard they tried, it didn't look like they could upset me (I hid my anger well, wouldn't you say?), they started cussing me.

I was handling all the foul words pretty well. That is, until they started reflecting negatively on my ancestry... in particular, about my mother. And, my friend, that is not a place you want to go with me.

Kinda hard to explain, but a calm came pouring over me, a very strange feeling for sure. I told Charlie I know this truck didn't have seat belts, so I suggested he'd better find something to hold onto.

I started reaching for the gears, and the down shifting began. Their previous pattern of behavior had showed that if I slow down, they will slow down. And that's exactly what I wanted them to do.

A little bit of a sidenote here: as far as I could tell, there was no one within 10 miles of us on this stretch of highway, just us and them.

Charlie looked at me with a panic on his face, screaming, "What are you doing? Donna, what are you doing?"

In as calm a voice as I could muster up, I replied, "Daddy always told me, when you see trash, you gather it up and take it out."

Suffice it to say, Charlie's mind must have figured out what I was about to do. After turning on my left blinker, because that's the law when you change lanes, I looked at him, smiled, and said, "I'm about to take the trash out."

Then I started changing lanes. Charlie was hollering at the top of his lungs, "You can't do that, you can't do that, you can't do that, you can't do that!"

I responded, "Calm down, my friend, I heard you the first time. Sit back, hide, and watch. I'm about to take the trash out!"

The only place this car full of ugly-talking trash could go was in the median, where it came to an abrupt stop. As we headed on into the yard, Charlie said, "Your Dad can't ever find out about this. I could get fired."

I kept looking forward and smiling... after a few seconds, I told him I agree.

You are probably wondering what happened to that car full of potty-mouth boys, and I can answer that for you. The one-ton truck that the rest of the crew rode in pulled into the yard about 30 minutes after we did. They were a little later leaving the jobsite than us, as they were picking up hand tools.

Charlie and I were starting to get a bit concerned, because back in these days, no cell phones. The men were getting out of the truck and started telling us why they were so late getting back to the yard. On their way in, they saw a car in the median with several young teenage boys standing around, looking very upset and clearly lost as a goose in a snowstorm. So, they stopped and asked them if they needed any help. Upon further inspection of the situation, they discovered the boys had two flats.

"When we asked what happened, they said some girl in a red Mack truck literally ran them off the road. So, we asked them, why would she do that? Finally, one of the boys spoke up and said, 'We may or may not have been messing with her.'"

While all the crew was standing there looking at me, I reached up in the truck and retrieved my work gloves out from under the seat, folded them, and put them in my back pocket as I was walking away. Feeling eyes on my backside, I stopped, turned around and said, "There are a lot of red Mack trucks on the road. It could have been anybody."

They turned and looked at Charlie, and Charlie shook his head saying, "I have no idea what y'all are talking about," as he turned and walked over to his car.

I hollered back, "Time to clock out, men, see y'all tomorrow!"

**Lesson learned:** *If you see a woman driving a big truck, for crying in a bucket, don't mess with her.*

# I don't know...

After stopping and listening to teenagers today, I realized my generation was not the only one to have "sayings." And by that, I mean those "catchy" little phrases that each generation is known for.

For me, and just about everyone at my high school, it was, "like, I don't know." Every question posed to me usually ended up with, "like, I don't know." To be truthful, I fully believe this is what my generation used as a comeback because we really didn't know the answer or what to say. Thinking back to high school makes me chuckle inside. Can you imagine what our teachers thought, especially the English teacher? Oh, my word!

Evidently, it became rather annoying to my Daddy, and it would seem on this day he'd had all he could take of my teenager sayings. I think his cup runneth over, but not in a good way, if you know what I mean. And to think, he had three of us kids to deal with at one time or another going through teenager antics and phraseology.

So, on purpose, he asked me a question, to which I immediately replied, "Like, I don't know."

And his response was hilarious: "Well, if you don't know, then who do we call to find out?" Talk about breaking me from sucking eggs! Seems like that was the last time I can ever remember using my teenager saying. Not really sure if he broke me of my teenager slang, or if it was a coincidence that I was outgrowing it.

Through the years, I can remember on occasion being out and about and hearing parents and their teenagers' conversations. Watching the looks on their parents' faces was too funny. Parents can have some pretty strange facial expressions, that's for sure. As I was taking it all in, I would just smile and let my mind drift back to those times with Daddy.

So, I must share something with you that happened recently. Since I have the privilege of being a high school rodeo team sponsor here in North Texas, I get to be around teenagers at our weekly rodeo meetings. And at a recent rodeo meeting, I started realizing this generation of teenagers also has a saying: "Like."

Everything they said started with the word "like." And that is when it hit me what my Daddy was talking about. This was annoying. Oh, my word, was it ever annoying!

But how do you get this into the teenagers' heads? It was hard for me to realize what my Daddy dealt with until this moment in time. Daddy helped me figure out how silly I sounded, so maybe I can help them figure out how silly they sound.

So, when the meeting began, I began every sentence with, "Like... who is calling this meeting to order?"

"Like... someone close the door."

"Like... who is calling roll?"

Are you getting my drift? Ha! All the parents busted out laughing. Heck, even the kids started laughing.

Anyway, finally one of the kids spoke up and said, "Miss Donna, do we really sound as stupid as you do?"

And it only took me a hot minute to answer them, *Yes! You do!*

Now, whether that makes a difference in the way they talk in the future is yet to be seen. I know that for the rest of the meeting, not one person began a sentence with "like." Guess they got the point I was making.

**Lesson learned:** *If you are ever in a conversation and don't know the answer, try some old teenager slang and answer back, "Like, I don't know."*

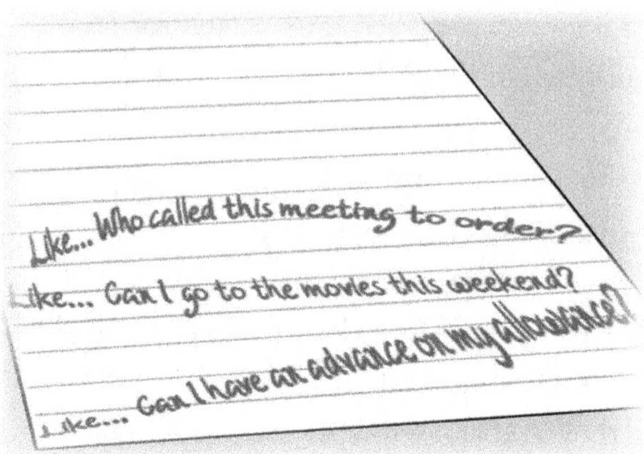

# I need some eye bleach...

Back in the middle '80s, I volunteered to take my mother, Grandma Gandee, and her sister, my Great Aunt Winnie, to Tennessee to see their sister-in-law, my Great Aunt Tommie. And no, I was not suicidal.

Out on the open road as we got into more rural areas with crops, Aunt Winnie and Grandma would start talking about their childhood growing up on the farm. Several of the stories, I had heard before, and some I had never heard. Aunt Winnie was so cute; when we passed a cotton field or bean patch, she would bend over with her hand on her back and say, "Ohhh, Edith, does your back hurt?"

Grandma would imitate her and exclaim back, "Oh, yes, ma'am. It does every time I look at a field that needs picking."

Then, they would laugh and laugh. They were reminiscing and acting like they were kids again. It was so cute to watch them in my rear-view mirror. A couple of times, I swear I saw two young girls sitting in the back seat just giggling.

Remember, this was before cell phones and navigation systems. Now, I can read a map. Daddy taught me well, and we found our way to her hometown. However, it helps when you have a telephone number.

I asked Mother if she had Aunt Tommie's home number, and she shook her head no and said, "I thought you had it."

Now, what? I was in the right town, but exactly where in this town does she live?

We all decided it would be best to pull over and figure out a plan. After pulling over in a parking lot, looking to my left I saw a phone booth. Depending on your age, you may or may not know what a phone booth is. If you don't, then Google it!

I stepped inside the phone booth and dialed the Operator. Didn't want everyone in the pickup to see how nervous I really was, so I kept my back to them. I figured if all else fails and the operator can't help me, I could call "collect" back to Daddy and get her number from him.

Something else Daddy taught me was to have a plan and at least one back-up plan. The Operator answered promptly, I told her my name and that I was all the way up from Texas to visit my Great Aunt Tommie, and I must have lost her phone number. She had married a man by the name of Mansel, and I kept rambling on with all sorts of information that I thought might be helpful.

Then I heard *click, click, click*. Suddenly, I heard Aunt Tommie's voice on the other end of the line. Hearing a familiar voice settled all my nerves down, and I could breathe a sigh of relief. Aunt Tommie gave really good directions, and we made it to her house in less than 10 minutes. She was so happy to see everyone from back home. I confided in Aunt Tommie what led up to me calling the operator for help.

She just smiled and winked at me. "Sweetie, living in a small town can have its perks. Everyone knows everyone, and everyone knows everyone's business."

I stood there staring at her, and she said, "Try saying that three times fast."

The next day, we all loaded up in my pickup and headed to the fabric store in town. Aunt Tommie wanted us to help her sew up a couple of new square-dancing outfits. Heading into town, I wanted to pass an eighteen-wheeler that was running in the left-hand lane and wouldn't get over, so I decided to pass it on the right-hand lane. Just as I pulled up beside the tractor trailer rig, something caught my eye, and I looked down on the bottom of the passenger's door where there was a little inset of glass. Kinda like a small window that didn't open.

This truck driver had a little male doll with its back side to the glass, and when he hit a button, the pants would drop down exposing his "blessed assurance." I saw that and thought, *Oh, my gosh, I hope no one else in the truck sees that.*

Too late... They were all pointing, cackling, and laughing. Eventually, we came home from town with some beautiful fabric and started working on those square-dancing skirts.

We had worked diligently all day, and at about 6 p.m., Aunt Tommie and I stopped cutting fabric, looked at each other, and almost at the same time said, "What's for supper?"

I spoke up and said, "Hey, we are on a little vacation. No cooking – let's go out to eat."

Everyone smiled and said, "Sounds like a plan to us."

Well, we had a little time to kill before heading into town for supper, and since there was only one bathroom in the house, it took a little while for all of us to get ready. Me, Aunt Winnie, Grandma, and Mother were all ready, so we were sitting in the living room waiting on Aunt Tommie.

Aunt Tommie said, "I will turn on a little TV. Y'all can watch while I finish getting ready. I have satellite now."

Now, this was when the satellite dishes were brand new out on the market, and this one was *huge* and took up a lot of yard space. This thing was at least 10 feet across, very massive.

Anyway, she turned on the TV, gave me a sheepish grin, and exited the room. Now, if you knew my Aunt Tommie, you would know by that look that she was up to something. Boy, howdy, was she.

We were all sitting there watching TV, excited to see something on satellite. Newest thing out on the market, and she had one.

At first, I thought, *This is a dumb movie.* The actors were not good at all. Grandma, Aunt Winnie, and Mother were talking amongst themselves about the actors not being very good. They would rather see John Wayne, Doris Day, or Clint Eastwood, just to name a few. And that is when I realized what Aunt Tommie had done.

The channel she put it on was, let's say, "X-rated," and I mean X-rated on steroids. A man broke through the door and saw the damsel in distress standing on the far wall of the room. Her hands were tied over her head, and she was crying, and it was the worst case of fake crying I have ever seem. Then, the would-be hero took off his trench coat, wearing nothing but his birthday suit and shoes. And oh, my gosh! I think you get the picture.

Grandma started screaming. Mother started screaming. Aunt Winnie started screaming. And here's me, sitting there and laughing watching them.

I was laughing so hard that I could barely walk as I ran around the room looking for the remote control to turn it off. And that's when I realized two things:

Aunt Tommie took the remote control with her.

Mother, Grandma, and Aunt Winnie while still screaming, never took their eyes off the TV.

Aunt Tommie came back into the room giggling and asked if anyone needed any eye bleach.

**Lesson learned:** *Keep the remote away from Aunt Tommie.*

# If common sense was lard, most people couldn't even grease a frying pan....

One summer, I was spending the weekend with Grandma Gandee, and we went over to Grannie's house, just a few miles down the road. Since Granddad had passed away, Grandma and Aunt Tommie were taking turns staying with Grannie at night so she could stay at home.

Grandma left her job of 13 years working for Fort Worth Laundry so she could help take care of her parents. Thus began the adventure of sewing more for the public like she used to do years ago.

I can remember stories that she told me about during WWII when she would sew prom dresses and wedding dresses out of parachute material. After looking at the pictures, you could have fooled me. They were absolutely beautiful. She said it was just like her momma use to say about just using good old common sense. Use what you have and don't make things overcomplicated. And that leads into my story...

On this day, Grandma and Aunt Tommie were working on a recent order they took in. Well, I was in the kitchen making myself a peanut butter and jelly sandwich. Got my bread, check; peanut butter, check; homemade jelly, big check. I opened the drawer to get a knife... and all the butter knives are gone.

What in the world? Did someone break in the house last night and steal all of Grannie's butter knives? *Hmmm*, things that make you go *hmmm*.

Well, I was so hungry, I took a spoon out of the drawer and used the back side of it to spread my peanut butter and jelly. With sandwich in hand, out of the kitchen I went, calling for Grandma.

As I was heading for the dining room, which is a straight shot from the kitchen, I stopped hollering and couldn't help but stare at the dining room table. There sat all the butter knives on the table. Mystery solved? Not so much solved as they had been found.

Now, it's time for an explanation as to how they got from the kitchen drawer to the dining room table. Then we'll get to the "why."

As I gazed at the table, my eyes saw patterns, fabric, scissors, pins, tape measures, and butter knives! A very strange combination if you ask me.

Anyway, Grandma and Aunt Tommie were busy laying out fabric on the dining room table. As I stood there, Grandma looked up and asked if I needed help with anything.

To which I replied, "I sure could had used one of those butter knives to fix my sandwich."

Grandma looked at Aunt Tommie, Aunt Tommie looked at me, then they both started laughing.

Grandma said, "You probably think this is a bit weird, but as necessity is the mother of invention, we came up with a new way to lay out a pattern."

I said, "Come again?"

"Donna, I will prove my point. When you went to make you a peanut butter and jelly sandwich, you were looking for a knife to spread everything with. Is that right?"

"Yes, ma'am, that's when I discovered all of Grannie's butter knives were missing, or at least I thought they were missing."

"Okay, so when you couldn't find a butter knife, what did you do?"

I said, "I did the only thing I could think to do – use the back side of a spoon to spread the peanut butter and jelly... Oh, wait a minute, I think I get what you are saying. I needed a knife, but couldn't find one, so out of necessity I figured out another way."

She just smiled at me.

Grandma went on to explain, "We figured out that it takes a lot of time to fit a pattern to fabric and be careful not to move the pattern as we pin a pattern to the fabric, so we had to come up with something to help things move faster. And we did! Instead of pinning the pattern, we lay heavyweight butter knives on the pattern. The heavyweight butter knives held the pattern in place and saved us time."

(Sidenote: Most people usually "pin" the pattern to the fabric. But not them, oh no. That takes too long.)

About that time, Grannie came in from outside and looked at the current situation on her dining room table and the perplexed look on my face. I looked up at her as she was taking the eggs out of her apron and setting them on the kitchen countertop. Never missing a step and continuing on with her task, she asked me if this was the first time I had ever seen someone cut out patterns like this.

To which I replied, "Yes, ma'am," and explained to her that my Home Economics teacher taught us to pin the pattern to the fabric.

Grannie laughed, telling me, "Child, don't always believe everything you are told. Why, if common sense was lard, there's a lot of people that couldn't even grease a frying pan."

**Lesson learned:** *If it works, it works.*

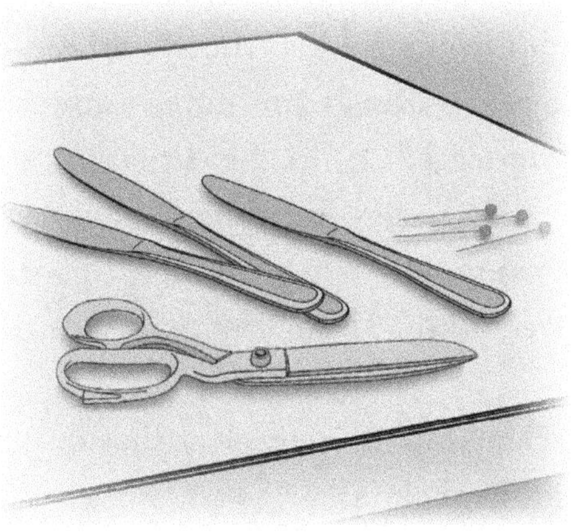

# If you can't take the heat, I suggest you get out of the kitchen...

This story is so old, Daddy would say it's older than black pepper. Many, many years back, Daddy and a few of his hunting buddies were up in Colorado on a deer hunt. They had been warned by some of the locals, as well as the Park Rangers, to be on the lookout for at least two men, and possibly a third, that had tried to rob other hunting parties. Rest assured; they were doing everything within their power tracking them down.

So, Daddy, Ted, Odelle, and another friend that I am not supposed to name (let's just call him Sal) was sitting in camp one night, bragging about the big bucks that they had seen earlier in the evening hunt. Supper was finished and everything was cleaned up and put away for the evening. Everyone was kicked back relaxing, drinking their coffee around the campfire when they heard something moving out in the trees.

When you are out in the wild, as they were, it is customary to keep your rifle or a side arm close, as you never know what might wander into camp, be it four-legged or, in this situation, two-legged trouble. Well, sure enough, here comes three men, all carrying deer rifles and walking into their camp. At first it all seemed innocent, until these three strangers started asking all sorts of questions that was really none of their business.

Of course, it became immediately clear that these were the men the Rangers had warned them about.

Not sure, but I think after hearing the story about these men from the Rangers at the beginning of their hunt, Daddy and his friends must had come up with a game plan just in case they ran into the would-be troublemakers. So, the games began…

Daddy spoke up first, introducing himself, then proceeded to introduce Ted. He began by saying, "This is Ted, and interesting enough, he only carries one bullet with him when he goes hunting."

One of the three strangers spoke up, and through his laughter said, "That's crazy. Why would you need only one bullet?"

To which Ted replied, "Because after being a Sniper in the military all those years, I never miss."

The stranger stopped laughing and asked, "Well, where is this 'one bullet?'"

To which Ted replied, "In the chamber. Just like me, always ready. Just like our motto, one shot, one kill."

Then Daddy turned to Odelle, who was sitting by the campfire, and asked him to introduce Sal.

Odelle said, "Well, sure, Harold. I will be glad to make the introductions."

Now, Sal was sitting on the ground by the campfire leaning against a stump, with his knife out and whittling on a stick.

"Men," Odelle said, "I would like for you to meet our friend, Sal. Rumor has it he ran with Al Capone back in the day and was a man that you just didn't want to make mad."

Well, the strangers immediately started looking at Sal sitting there, realizing he had never said a word the whole time. Sal stopped whittling long enough to look up at the strangers, and with a straight face, took his pocketknife and stabbed it into his leg. The strangers gasped like they couldn't catch their breath.

On Sal's face was a cold hard look as if the knife in his leg only felt like a mosquito bite. Sal reached with both hands and pulled the knife out, looking straight at the would-be robbers and said, "If you can't take the heat, I suggest you get out of the kitchen." Then, without missing a beat, he went back to whittling.

One of the strangers went to throwing up, one started crying, and the third man started backing up and apologizing for disturbing the camp. They liked to have knocked each other down getting away from Daddy and his friends' hunting camp. Daddy said they never saw them the rest of the hunting trip.

Oh, yeah, I guess I had better explain myself… What those three strangers didn't know was that Sal had a wooden leg, and yes, you guessed it, that was the leg he stabbed his pocketknife into. But hey, those three would-be bad men didn't know that, did they?

**Lesson learned:** *If you can't take the heat, I suggest you get out of the kitchen.*

# I'm gonna have to head home now...

To start with, I have to let everyone know that my Daddy, "Daddy Snow" as everyone calls him, is a very old school kinda guy. And when I say old school... I mean *old school.*

You didn't cuss women or children, and you certainly didn't make "off-colored" jokes in mixed company. This was also back in the time when, if you were a "young man" and you broke these rules, you got your mouth washed out with lye soap. The same lye soap all the moms and grandmothers made. I would have loved to be a fly on the wall and seen that, how about you?

I remember Grandma Snow and Grandma Gandee both talking about growing up and how when any of their brothers "broke the rules," look out! Lye soap was inserted in their mouths and pulled out scraping up against the back side of their top teeth. Oh, my gosh! If anyone did that today, it would probably be considered child abuse. So, Daddy grew up back in what some call "the good old days."

Anyway, back to my story about Daddy...

We were at a Texas Flip N Move watch party at our favorite BBQ place down in the historic Fort Worth Stockyards, and everyone was having such a great time. Mother and Daddy would normally get there about one and a half hours early because they were afraid the restaurant might run out of food. I tried to reassure them they would not, but Daddy insisted, and who am I to argue with him? I may be stubborn, just like him, but I am a quick learner. Do not argue with Daddy; just do as he says, unless you want to see Jesus early in life.

On this Friday night, we were watching the newest episode, laughing, and having so much fun. During the commercial breaks, we would always do door prizes and take any questions. Then, after the show was over, Toni, Randy, and I would stick around for any additional questions, pictures, and autographs.

I almost forgot, it was on this night that Randy kept picking on me and Toni. And I mean every chance he got, there was another little "jab" or "dig." He was in rare form, that was for sure. As a rule, dealing with Randy is about like water rolling off a duck's back with me. Never had a problem looking him in the eye and letting everything he said go in one ear and out the other, smiling the whole time. But this night was different.

I took it and took it and then something snapped. The only way I can describe it is, it was like he had just pitched a tent on my last nerve.

As I was walking back up to the front of the room so we could draw tickets for a door prize, I realized Randy was hot on my heels. Something came over me, and I stopped dead in my tracks. I wheeled around, and there was Randy, almost nose to nose with me.

I put my finger in his chest, started walking him backwards, and said, "Looky here, scooter. I can unload 50-pound sacks of horse feed, throw 65-pound bales of hay, control a 1200-pound horse, and bring him to the ground if he makes me mad. You, sir, will not be a problem. Do I make myself clear?"

For the first time since I have known him, he was speechless. Randy just stood there. His mouth was moving but nothing was coming out. Almost like the lights are on, but nobody's home.

It would appear my facial expression matched my tone of voice. So, I reached up and gently tapped him on his right cheek, smiled, and said, "Good, we have an understanding. Now, back off, buck-o."

For the rest of the evening, Randy walked a big circle around us, and that suited me just fine.

Back to the story. On this particular day, we had moved a large historical house, and all of us were very physically tired but on an adrenaline rush at the same time. I suspect this was from the excitement for the watch party. Glancing over at Daddy towards the end of the episode, I could tell he was sinking fast. As a matter of fact, even with all the noise, he was nodding off. He had a long day too. So, in his own special way, he needed to let me know that him and Mother were gonna head on out and go home before the evening's festivities were over.

I was on the microphone answering a question when Daddy approached me. And being the dutiful daughter that I am, I quickly turned my attention to him. As I turned toward Daddy, I completely forgot the microphone was still on.

He looked at me through his sleepy eyes and said, "Me and your Mother are gonna head on home."

I said, "Yes, sir, whatever you need to do."

He was walking away and quickly turned, came back to me, and said, "Donna, the truth is, I need to take your Mother home. She can't keep her hands off me."

I just stood there with my mouth hanging open.

In case you were wondering, everyone in the room overheard him on the microphone and was rolling on the floor, laughing hysterically. I was laughing so hard I could hardly catch my breath.

Does Daddy Snow know how to make an exit, or what?

**Lesson learned:** *Be prepared, and hold onto your seat. You never know what will come out of Daddy Snow's mouth.*

# Just as sure as you're a foot tall!

Do you remember when you got your first car to drive to school? Do you remember starting to "butter your parents up" when you got your learner's permit?

Actually, I put a whole lot of strategy into my plan. But my plan didn't work out exactly as I had hoped for! One evening, Daddy came home from work and said he had a surprise for me. Well, who doesn't like surprises, right?

Jumping up and down, I hollered, "Where is it, where is it?"

By the grin on Daddy's face, I could tell he was very excited himself. He said, "It's right outside on the trailer."

*Trailer?* As I went out the back door of the house, there it was. It was a Jeep!

For the most part, Dads are pretty doggone smart, and mine was no exception. Figuring he could get two birds with one stone, he bought the Jeep from a friend with the intent of letting me drive it to school, and he could take it on hunting trips.

I was mad! I wanted a pickup. So, Daddy did the only thing he could.

He said, "Well, as I see it, you have two options here... either drive the Jeep to school or walk. The choice is yours. Think it over and let me know what your decision is."

You know that was the longest 30 seconds of my life. I may have been born at night, but it wasn't last night. I quickly turned that frown into a smile and said, "I believe I will take option one!"

And that is where this story begins...

Back in high school, I drove a 1964 Willis Jeep that was painted baby blue. At first, I didn't think I was gonna like it, but I ended up loving it. My Daddy was only the second owner. It was baby blue and had a winch on the front as well as on the back. Then, when I started making a lot of money with it pulling people out of ditches, that's about the time I started liking it.

One day at high school, we were coming back from lunch. That was when you were allowed to actually leave campus for lunch. Well, I parked in my usual parking space out in the front parking lot. As we crossed the street, I could see Principal Hagman standing at the head of the front steps, which was the main entrance to the building. Now, you have got to understand that Principal Hagman was a big man that stood around 6'6" or more. As a matter of fact, the rumor around the school was he had actually retired from playing professional football. Trust me, if you saw him, you would think so too!

Anyway, as we were walking up the steps, I could feel his eyes on me. Now, I knew I was back in plenty of time to get to class. I shouldn't be in trouble, right? The best way to describe the feeling I felt was that same feeling when you're driving down the road, see a police officer, you suck wind, and immediately hit your brakes. Then, you realize you weren't even speeding to start with! Yeah, that feeling.

As I walked past him, thinking I was in the clear, I hear my name being called... *Donna Snow.*

Of course, being raised the way I was, I knew to immediately turn around and acknowledge him with, "Yes, sir?"

He proceeds to ask me if I am proud of my "little blue Jeep," to which I respond, "Well, yes, sir, I am."

He then asked me if I thought my "little blue Jeep " could climb the front steps of the high school.

It was at this point that my mouth engaged before my brain, and I said, "Just as sure as you're a foot tall, it sure can!"

He laughed and said, "Prove it!"

Quickly, I came to my senses and explained that would be against school policy, and I didn't want to get in trouble. I have to tell you, I grew up during a time that when you got in trouble at school, you got in trouble again when you got home for getting in trouble at school. Can I get a witness?

Principal Hagman started grinning and laughing. He went on to say that he was the Principal and what he says goes! I stood there in silence, not really knowing what to say next. I truly think he knew I was uneasy, and again, he challenged me to prove it.

So, my lightning-fast mind asked, "If I do, am I gonna get in trouble?"

He said, "Not only will you not get in trouble, but if you can put that Jeep at the top of the steps, I will give you an excused absence for the rest of the day."

It does not take long for me to look at a hot baked potato, so I accepted his challenge.

I turned and walked down the steps, walked across the street, and got in my little blue Jeep and fired her up! Once I came out of the parking lot and lined up with the steps, I threw it down in the "low hole" and even turned my hubs to four-wheel drive.

Now, for those of you who own a Jeep or a four-wheel drive vehicle, you may be thinking, *that was a little bit of an overkill.* And you would be right. But at the ripe old age of 16, I was not taking any chances. I figured it this way: if I messed up and got in trouble with the principal, then I would get in trouble at home, which could lead to me being grounded for the next 20 years. Nope... I was not taking any chances.

Well, I took a deep breath, eased up on the curb, crossed the sidewalk, and prepared to climb the mountain of steps to victory. Step by step, I climbed all the way to the top until I was on the same level as where the challenge was issued.

Obviously, at this point, I was pretty proud of myself and my little blue Jeep. True to his word, Principal Hagman gave me a pass for the rest of the day.

**Lesson learned:** *Always mind your elders. You never know what the reward may be!*

# Let me guess; you were born on the side of a hill, and the door just slammed shut?

Growing up, was I the only kid that had trouble remembering to turn off lights once you left a room and shut doors properly?

I truly believe that our parents overlooked "this issue" many a time when we were little kids, because we couldn't reach the light switch, nor did we have enough "lead in our britches" to open and close a door. But then the day came when playtime was over and there was a new set of rules to go by.

The house we grew up in started out as a small two-bedroom, one bath, kitchen, and living room with a single car garage that Daddy moved for us to Haltom City. I was in the 1st grade. Daddy would clean lumber that was discarded on various jobs and bring it home in the back of his pickup.

Over a period of time, with the lumber he cleaned and stored along with the lumber given to him and what he purchased, he began to add on to our humble abode. When he finished, our house grew to a six-bedroom, three bath, family den, kitchen, laundry room with a food pantry, music room, game room, and last but not least, Daddy's hunting library. Trust me, it was all there.

How do I know? Because I had to help clean it! Our back door was a sliding glass door, and Daddy always made sure the tracks were working good. His secret was a candle. As he rubbed the wax off of a candle onto the track itself, it would roll as smoothly as if it was brand new. So, in my defense, I guess you could say it wasn't totally my fault. I think Daddy should take at least a little of the blame. Let's talk about the door first.

You know when it's Saturday, and after doing your chores, it's time to go play?

So, everyone heads outside to play. Well, I was the last one out the door and so glad we could finally go play. I guess I accidentally tried shutting the door too fast or too hard. So, the end result was it slammed shut and bounced back open a little bit. Well, I was too busy to slow down and make sure it was "shut properly."

It seems I wasn't the only one. Toni and Gary seemed to have the same problem too. Was it just us? Or did you ever have this problem?

So, needless to say, all three of us started getting in trouble repeatedly. Must have gotten to the point that Daddy was tired of constantly telling us to make sure the door was shut.

Daddy came up with a plan... and the plan eventually worked.

So, when we would run out the back door and "accidentally" not make sure it was closed properly, Daddy would holler out at us, "Were you born on the side of the hill and the door just slammed shut?"

He would make us come back and open and shut the door several times. Then, I guess the point was really driven in when we had to do it in front of our friends. To be honest, I think the embarrassment of getting in trouble in front of our friends did the trick.

And now, to the light switches. This problem was mostly in our bedrooms. As an adult that pays electric bills, I totally get the premise of "when you leave a room, turn the light switch off." But when you don't pay the electric bill, it can be harder to remember.

We must have pushed Daddy to the point of no return, so he came up with something that he felt would really get my attention. One night after work, he sat me down and said, "I'm going to talk to you like a young adult."

That made me feel grown up; he had my undivided attention.

Bottom line – he would give me two warnings to either remember to turn the light switch off when I left my bedroom or loose the light bulb. Since I was a scaredy cat of the dark to start with, this got my attention. Funny how consequences can change your thinking, isn't it?

What is it they say? Daddy knows best.

**Lesson learned:** *If on the off chance you weren't born on the side of a hill and the door always slammed shut, stop and make sure the door is shut properly and not slammed so you aren't embarrassed in front of your friends.*

*And for crying in a bucket, remember to turn lights off when you leave a room. Good practice for when you grow up and have to pay the electric bill.*

# Look out the cows are in with the chickens...

Even though I couldn't have been more than seven or eight years old, my memory is very vivid of that day, almost to the point of needing therapy.

Daddy, Mother, Gary, Toni, and I, along with many members of our family, were over at Grannie Graves' house on a Sunday for a family gathering. This was something that we did several times a year, carving out time and spending it with our family. Since there was a lot of us there, this called for a big spread for lunch.

Mother, Aunt Shorty, Grandma Gandee, and Grannie were all over the little shotgun-style kitchen cooking up a mess of vittles. The most heavenly smells filled the room and traveled throughout the house. Why, you could even smell it down in the bathroom. The kitchen itself was long and narrow and only so many people could move around, so they set me on the kitchen stool in the doorway, so I wouldn't be getting "underfoot," as they called it.

Grandma Gandee was tending to the chicken frying in the cast iron skillet, and Mother was cooking the corn, black eyed peas, and cutting up taters to fry with onions. Aunt Shorty was deviling the eggs, slicing homemade pickles, and cutting up salads. Grannie had just taken the homemade yeast rolls out of the oven when she decided she had better make another cake for dessert. Evidently four just wasn't enough. Man, Grannie sure could put on the feed bag. Grannie always said, if you leave this house hungry, it's your own fault. Always, more than enough food was cooked, which meant we could take leftovers home. *Yum, yum.*

She looked into her "icebox" – yes, that is what she called it – and guess what? Not enough eggs. Grannie looked up and said, "Well, that will never do."

So, she announces she is gonna run out to the hen house and gather a few eggs in order to make her fifth cake. Well, when I heard that, I jumped down off the stool and hollered, "Can I go, can I go, too, Grannie?"

Grannie smiled and said, "Come on, child. Yes, you can go."

I was so excited! Grannie handed me the egg basket, and then off to the hen house we went. Well, we rounded the corner and went in the outside area through the chicken wire door. But when we went into the roosting area, where we would find the eggs we needed, there was all sorts of commotion going on. Hens were squawking and flying all over the place. Straw and dust were flying everywhere. Grannie grabbed me and pulled me behind her and said, "Stay behind me."

I was a shaking in my shoes and trying to figure out what was going on all at the same time.

It was about this time that amongst all the chickens squawking and dust flying that I heard a lot of very distinct *mooooing*. Yes, sir, you heard me right. *Mooooing* in a chicken house.

Needless to say, curiosity was definitely getting the best of me. So, I peeked around Grannie's dress, and what did I see? Cows!

Grannie stood there looking at them, and they were looking back at her. Most definitely, the cows were as shocked as Grannie was.

Grannie reached down, grabbed my hand, and was literally all but dragging me behind her. I was thinking Grannie must be scared, 'cause I knew I was.

Well, I was wrong. She wasn't scared, she was mad. And I mean *mad.* She was madder than a hornet's nest that had just been hit with a stick. Evidently, Granddad Graves hadn't gotten his "honey-do list of chores" done before everyone arrived. Anyone want to take a wild guess what was on the list to do? Well, if you guessed fence repair, you would be right.

Into the house we went. Now, my Grannie was a big woman, standing right at 6-feet tall, and she was getting madder by the minute. So, my little feet were doing double time. No sooner than the screen door slammed behind me, Grannie started hollering for Granddad.

"Carl, Carl... Where are you? You better speak up right now! This is important."

Grandad hollered and said, "Here I am in the living room."

Grannie stormed in there and hollered, "Look out the cows are in with the chickens. And if you want to eat lunch, I suggest you and the rest of the men folk be doing something about it!"

It was easy to see that you just didn't mess around with my Grannie. When she said to jump, the only response was, "Yes, ma'am. How high?"

Granddad looked at the menfolk in the room and announced, "Seems like if we want to eat, we best get the cows out of the hen house and the fence fixed."

So, out the door they all went. Since there were so many of them, that fence was fixed faster than you could snap your fingers. As they were coming back in the house, Grannie was hollering, "Go wash up! We are setting lunch on the table, less the fifth cake."

**Lesson learned:** *When your wife gives you a honey-do list, I strongly suggest you do it in a timely manner. If you don't, then your family may see you get a tongue lashing or your legs whipped!*

# Never miss an opportunity to sow a seed by helping someone...

Daddy always taught us to never miss out on a chance to lend a helping hand. It's like planting good seed in the ground. Hang around, and a harvest will come up.

It was getting late in the day. There was a bad storm blowing in, and Daddy was trying to get back to the yard before the brunt of the bad weather hit.

The big pull truck he was driving was "Big Mama," and he had her wound-up heading in. He noticed that the traffic started slowing down and was trying to figure out what was going on.

As he got closer, he could make out a pickup off in the bar ditch to his right. Seems as though people were what we call "rubber necking," just trying to see what was going on, yet not stopping to offer any help.

If you had ever met my Daddy, one thing you would know is he never missed a chance to lend a helping hand. You noticed I did not say a "handout"; I said a "hand up."

Evidently, this man had hydroplaned right off the road and into the bar ditch, and as much as he was waving at people, no one would stop to help him. They'd only look at him and keep on driving.

Daddy pulled over in his big truck, and he said the bottom was starting to fall out of the sky as he got out. Wind started picking up, and the rain was getting heavier.

He hollered at the guy down in the ditch, "Let's get you up out of there before the bad stuff hits!"

The man waved his hand in agreement.

Daddy reached up on the winch and threw the brake off so he could pull out enough winch line to get down to the pickup. With enough line now to the pickup, he hollered to the man to hook it up, get in the cab, and keep the tires straight. The man did as Daddy instructed, and within a few minutes, the pickup was up out of the ditch and back on the road.

Daddy set his air brakes, climbed down out of the cab, and was undoing the winch line off the pickup before the man could get out of his truck.

Once the winch line had been rolled back up, the man walked up to Daddy, profusely thanking him for stopping to help and tried to give him money. Seems as if he had been down in the ditch for quite a while, and no one stopped to help him.

Daddy introduced himself and said, "No, sir, I don't want your money. I'm just glad I was able to help." They shook hands and parted ways.

So, the man drove off in one direction and Daddy in the other, heading to the yard.

Many years later, Daddy received a phone call to look at a house to be moved. He went and ran the route out, called the prospective customers, and said they had one problem. The only route to get the house to its new location was via a really bad corner. The equipment they had back then was not what we have today. Today, the corner would have not been an issue.

Seems the man who owned the pasture was... well, let's say he was not liked very much by the community. Evidently, he was known for having a cold heart.

Daddy met with the young couple wanting to have the house moved and told them they'd need to get permission to cross a pasture, as the corner could not be made. The rest of the route was great; it was just this corner. He told them that he would need to take down two small pieces of fence, cross the corner of the pasture, and put the pieces back up.

The young couple looked at each other and said, "The man who owns this pasture, we are told, is very cold-hearted and not known for helping anyone." The wife started crying, the husband standing there wringing his hands.

Daddy could see the stress all over their faces.

"How about this?" Daddy said. "Let me go up and see if I can make a deal with the man about letting us cross his pasture. You folks need to calm down. Have faith."

Daddy pulled into the driveway of the owner's house and could clearly see him sitting on the front porch watching him closely.

Getting out of the pickup, Daddy put on his best smile and walked towards the front porch. He introduced himself to the man and asked if he could visit with him for a few minutes. The man on the porch nodded his head yes.

Daddy explained the situation about the young couple, that this was their chance to get a home and begin their life together. He went on to explain the corner and fence situation.

Daddy assured him, "We will take the fences down, cross the pasture, fill in any ruts, and put the fences back up good as new."

The old man leaned forward in his chair, looking Daddy straight in the eyes and said, "Son, I will give you permission to cross my pasture. However, don't you touch my fence, and if you leave ruts, I will tend to them and then I will put the fences back up."

Daddy was shocked and told the man he appreciated the help.

The old man said, "You don't remember me, do you, son?"

To which Daddy said, "No, sir, I'm sorry. I don't."

"Well, son, it's been about 25 years ago now. Out on an old county road, a bad storm was coming in, and you were the only one who would stop and help me." For the first time, the old man smiled and said, "Now, I get a chance to lend a helping hand."

Well, Daddy went back down the road to where he had left the young couple standing by their car. He explained that the man had given permission. Daddy found out later that they had become friends with the old man and shared many fun times up until his death.

**Lesson learned:** *We are told 365 times in the Bible not to worry, one for each day of the year. So, don't worry. Don't waste your time and energy worrying about something. It won't help – not one little bit. It will rob you of peace. Take Daddy Snow's advice. Never miss a chance to sow a seed by helping someone.*

# No one wants to hear a boring story...

Back in my late teens and early twenties, I became infatuated with CB radios. Looking back, I can see where the CB radio grew in popularity during this time period.

One of the first things that got my attention was all the different "handles" the truck drivers had, like a catchy or cute name. Most everyone had a handle, as they didn't use their first or last names on the radio. As I made friends with some of the drivers, men and women both, I asked why they chose to use "handles" and not their first name.

Seems there are two schools of thought on this subject. Some truckers have long hauls, and let's be honest, you can only listen to the radio or music for so long. Sometimes, you just need that human interaction, and this made sense to me.

However, some of them didn't want their wife or husband to know they were in town. I was like, "That doesn't make any since. Why wouldn't they want their wife or husband to know they were in town?"

Their response was, "Well, hypothetically, some men could be hiding their wife from their girlfriend, and some women could be hiding their husband from their boyfriend, or vice versa."

"Ohhhh," was my answer. Now I get it. No more explanations needed here.

Therefore, since their voice did become a little distorted over the radio, it was easy to hide their identity. Now, let's get something straight here – not all truck drivers did this to their spouse. Some do… most don't.

I truly had a blast on my CB radio talking to truck drivers as they came through my hometown of Fort Worth, Texas. In the beginning, it was overwhelming trying to learn all their truck-driving lingo. Everything they said had a definite meaning.

Such as, after a couple of them would finish their conversation, one of them would say, "This here is Rocket Man, and I am on the side," meaning that he had finished with his part of the conversation on the radio, but still listening just in case someone else wanted to talk to him.

Or, "This is Blue Blazes signing off. Pulling in at this choke and puke, taking a 10–100 and a 10–200."

Now, a choke and puke was an eating establishment, and the 10–100 / 10–200… Well, I'll let you figure that one out.

There were some really cool handles. Let's see if I can remember some of them for you. There was, Red Hot, Rambling Man, China Doll, Chatty Cathy, Roadkill, Prancing Palomino, Hot Momma, and Snow Man just to mention a few, and the one this story revolves around is Hacksaw.

It was through a father, mother, and son truck-driving family that I met him.

Now, Hacksaw was an older man that, as he put it, "had seen a lot of hard miles." Seems he deemed himself a professional truck driver. He was kinda rough around the edges; you never knew what was gonna come out of his mouth. However, he seemed to have a heart of gold, which was a very unusual combination. And come to think of it, through all the years that I knew him, up to this point in time, I never heard him talk of a Mrs. Hacksaw. *Hmm.*

Anyway, I wanted to tell you a little story that Hacksaw shared with a few of us one night. There were several of us sitting around at a coffee shop late one evening down at the truck stop. A few of our friends had just come in off the road to fuel up, eat a good hot meal, and take a break before heading out for their destination. And just like all the times in the past, everyone was waiting on the newest story from Hacksaw. Puts me in mind of a family reunion, with the favorite uncle at the center of attention. No one could tell a story any better than he could.

Seemed like the time was right. All the trucking family was gathering around Hacksaw, trying to find the most comfortable seats in the café booths and surrounding tables, because the next order of business was story time. A café that once buzzed with everyone talking and clanging of spoons on coffee cups became as quiet as a graveyard. No one uttered a sound. Now that I think about it, it was kinda like Christmas, sitting there with anticipation and waiting for someone to pass out the gifts.

Hacksaw took his place. We all were sitting there as quiet as a church mouse, and when he knew he had our undivided attention, he began to speak. Looking like a judge, he sat up very straight in his chair as if commanding his court room.

First words out of his mouth: "I want everyone in this room to know that I have a wife who would do anything I told her to do, any time I told her to."

We all looked at him and pretty much at the same time said, "You have a wife?"

He just laughed and said, "Doesn't every man?" He then cleared his throat and said, "Do you want to hear this story or not?" He boomed this warning out like a judge in a court room.

"Yes, yes, yes, please go on!" we all exclaimed. No one wanted Hacksaw to stop now. It was getting really good!

He then proceeded to tell us that he had her on her hands and knees last night. Well, we all looked at each other, and you could tell by the look on everyone's face that we were all thinking, *Do we really want to hear this story?* To which we all shrugged our shoulders and begged him to go on.

"As I was saying," Hacksaw went on to say, "my wife does what I tell her to, any time I tell her to. Like just last night, I had her on her hands and knees."

To which we all replied, "Whoa!"

Hacksaw looked each one of us in the eye, and in his undeniable authoritative voice said, "Do you want to know what she said?"

Of course, we all wanted to know, but then again, this was Hacksaw. There was a 50/50 chance that his stories would either make us fall in the floor laughing or sit there with our mouths standing wide open catching flies. Evidently, this night we had all decided to live on the wild side of life, and braced ourselves for what was about to come next.

We gave in and said, yes, we wanted to know. Just like in Hacksaw fashion, he smiled and prepared to tell the punch line.

"Yep, I had her on her hands and knees last night... Guess what she said?"

Silence fell over the crowd of people, and not only us. Everyone else within ear shot distance of Hacksaw wanted to hear. Now was the moment of truth; we had come this far, no going back now.

*No, sir, we were all in this together*, I said to myself. *I am not gonna be the one who asks what she said.*

We all sat there, in hopes that someone would speak up and ask what she said.

Finally, someone did, and I think it was Red Hot (that's his handle).

He said, "What did she say, what did she say?"

To which Hacksaw replied in a loud booming voice, "Come out from underneath that bed, you coward!"

Everyone busted out laughing, as this had to be the best story he had ever told.

After we all had a good laugh, people started dispersing, picking up their thermoses the waitresses had filled with coffee, and going back to their trucks to head on down the road.

As everyone was saying their goodbyes, I tarried behind, so I could talk to Hacksaw.

He saw me standing there and said, "Hey, China Doll, you heading home?"

I said, "Yes, sir, getting late and I have work tomorrow. But may I ask you a question?"

He nodded his head yes.

"Hacksaw, why do you tell such wild stories?"

To which he replied, "Darling, always remember – no one wants to hear a boring story."

**Lesson learned:** *Yes, my handle was China Doll. But more importantly, I learned to slow down. Don't let life get you all in a rush, always wait for the end of the story as it just might make you laugh, and if you ever run into Hacksaw, be prepared to be amazed.*

# Now, go tell your friends...

As far back as I can remember, throughout the summer and into the fall, we always helped Grandma Gandee work her, as she referred to it, "small garden."

And oh, yes, by the way, her idea of a small garden was a little over two-acres! When asked why she had such a big garden, her answer was always the same: "Because we want to make sure our family has good food to not only eat now, but also enough to carry them through the winter."

Truth be told, in the beginning of my years working the garden, I didn't like it. A lot of work throughout the day, and not enough time to play.

Throughout the summer and into fall, almost every weekend there was something to pick from the garden. Even though, sometimes as a young kid, I complained about working long hours in the garden or in a hot kitchen canning the food, I was always glad when it came wintertime and we had yummy vegetables to eat. I began to have pride in the fact that we grew our own food, processed it, and canned it.

As I grew older, I still loved the fresh vegetables from her garden, but more than that, I loved the time I spent with her, my sister, and my mother. Okay, I will add my brother in there too.

One of my favorite things to pick was the bell tomatoes. I had come up with a special way of picking bell tomatoes, and I thought I was being really sneaky. You pick one, you eat one.

When we were working those rows, one day out of nowhere, Grandma Gandee told me, "It's okay on the bell tomato isles to pick three or four, then eat one."

Thinking that I had been caught, I confessed to her that I was picking one and eating one.

She laughed and said, "Do you think you're the first person to pick like that?"

I looked over at her and asked, "You picked like that too?"

"Yes, ma'am, I did, until I realized that eating too many of them can give you the 'back-door trots,' and the bathroom is never as close as you wish it was."

We both laughed out loud and went back to work. When I think back on those years, I realized she really did make working in the garden fun.

One morning, as we were walking down to the garden to work, I told Grandma that her garden was so pretty with all the marigolds she had planted and the different rows of different colors. It looked just like a picture postcard.

She said marigolds serve two purposes. One is that they are very pretty and colorful. However, the main reason is they helped keep bugs out of her garden. Wow, I didn't know that. So, if you ever decide to put in a garden, be sure to plant some marigolds.

As the different vegetables were ready for picking, there we stood, ready to take the bounty and reap the benefits of all our hard work.

From shelling black-eyed peas and snapping green beans to silking corn under the big oak tree at the end of her garage and taking them into the house to be canned... These are all precious memories. To be honest with you, sometimes I wish I could go back to those days. Times were less chaotic, and the food was out of this world.

Next, we went in the house and started canning our treasures. After everything was canned, we would listen for the *pop*, which told us they had properly sealed. If you happen to have several jars seal at the same time, you could have sworn it was a machine gun going off.

Anyway, so much for going down memory lane. Time to get back to my story.

We were working in the garden one Saturday morning, gathering peas to shell, when out of nowhere, for the first time, I heard Grandma say, "Now, go tell your friends."

Or at least, I thought it was her. I looked up to see who she was talking to, but no one was there, and Grandma was looking down and picking peas. So, I thought to myself, maybe I just thought I heard her say something. I went back to picking.

A few minutes later, I heard the same thing. So, I stopped and looked her way again. Truth be told, Grandma was... how do I say this? An "older" lady or an "experienced" lady? What the heck, I'm just gonna say it. I thought she was a little bit shy of a full quart! There, I said it!

I stood up and looked at her and asked, "Who are you talking to?"

Grandma told me she was talking to a grasshopper!

I looked at her and said, "Come again?"

She laughed that laugh that I can still recall today. Calling me over to her, I saw her bend down and pick up something in her hand. As I approached her, I could see she had a grasshopper.

When I walked up to her, she said to me, "Watch."

So, as I stood there, she pulled the head off of the grasshopper and said to it, "There, now go tell your friends about this place!"

Needless to say, this young girl was definitely confused... more than usual. Evidently, the look on my face was, in fact, a look of confusion.

I said, "Grandma, if you pull their heads off, how can they hear what you're saying, much less go tell their friends?"

Grandma said, "I guess that did sound crazy," and she started laughing at me. She laughed so much, I thought she was gonna pee her pants.

Well, you know how it goes. When someone's funny bone is tickled, it becomes contagious. We were laughing so hard, we literally fell down to the ground.

Now enters Papaw Gandee.

He walks by us, going to get on his tractor to finish working the bottom part of the garden, and without missing a step, he says, "You women folk have gone and lost your minds, but I would appreciate it if you could find it before lunch. I am powerfully hungry."

**Lesson learned:** *Just because someone is "older" doesn't mean they can't have a sense of humor. And by the way, any chance you get, pass her lesson on, laughter is always good, even if you're killing grasshoppers!*

# Oh, fiddle sticks...

Just in case you haven't guessed by now, I was a tomboy growing up. Now, don't misunderstand. If the occasion calls for it, I can clean up pretty doggone good, even if I do say so myself.

While Daddy did teach me at an early age the basics of how to drive the 1964 Mack, "Big Bad John," on the job site and work the wench, he never let me out on the street with it. So, now that I was older, I decided it was time for me to learn to drive the truck on the street.

Now, Daddy always taught us kids by "hands on." That way, you learn very quickly what to do, but maybe more importantly, what *not* to do.

As it turned out, Daddy was way covered up with work and really didn't have the time to help me, so I turned to Pop. When I asked for help in learning to drive the 1964 Mack on the street, Pop said he would do it if Daddy gave his permission.

So, after promising Daddy all of Texas and half of Georgia (sorry, Georgia, it's an old saying which means I promised him everything I could think of), he agreed. Daddy was quick to tell me it's very different than driving around on the job site. Just to make her untrack, you had to know what to do with those three gear sticks – the main five, auxiliary behind that, and a brown lipe behind that. That's a five, four and four. If you don't understand that lingo, find a truck driver to explain it or come by the office and I will show you.

I figured, how hard could it be? I have a working understanding of the gear sticks. So, really, how hard could it be? Right? Well, I was about to find out.

I was excited to tell Pop that Daddy gave his permission.

"So, when can we start? When can we start? When can we start?"

Can you tell I was excited? Pop said we had to sit down and have a real good understanding as to how this teacher/student thing was gonna work.

"First, you have to work through all gears without grinding them, and there will be no crying. When I tell you to stop and start over, don't back talk me. Do just like I tell you. Driving this truck or any truck with these many gears comes down to one thing – practice, practice, practice. And that wasn't gonna happen on the first driving lesson. Agreed?"

"Yes, sir, I agree." This meant if I messed up one time, just one time, I had to stop and put everything all back down in first gear and start all over.

I guess you could look at this meeting kinda like an orientation of sorts. It seems we had talked so long (well, really, Pop was doing all the talking) that I just sat there, smiled, nodded yes, and said, "Yes, sir," a whole lot.

Pop decided it was too late in the day to start, so tomorrow right after work, the teaching would begin. While I was not happy with his decision, I knew getting upset would not be in my best interest. So, I gritted my teeth, smiled, and said, "Yes, sir, tomorrow it is."

As you can imagine, tomorrow couldn't get here fast enough for me. Honestly, I don't think I even slept that night. Anticipation was almost too much for me to bear. Come to think of it, seems to me I showed up for work two hours early the next morning. My teenage mind was reasoning that the sooner I got to work, the sooner the workday would be over, and the sooner I could get behind the wheel and out on the road. And just like that, nine hours later, it was quitting time, which meant it was almost time to start my first driving lesson on the street. I was one happy girl!

Walking up to the truck, I was reminded about how much pride my Daddy has in his equipment. This truck was always kept very clean and shiny. He had a rule for whoever was driving: you use the little hand whisk broom to sweep out the floorboards twice a day, once after lunch and once at the end of the workday. "John," as we referred to the truck, was the most beautiful candy apple red you have ever seen. Why, it was so shiny, you could even part your hair by looking in the paint, just as good as a mirror.

The last time Daddy had this truck painted, the painter suggested an unusual method to give this candy apple red finish a luster that everyone would be envious of.

This peaked Daddy's interest, and he said, "Tell me about it."

"Well, H.D., I know you don't care anything for alcohol, but the secret to my painting method is adding beer."

Daddy stood there for a few minutes before looking up, smiling, and said, "Do you add the beer to you or the paint?"

They both laughed and he said, "Oh no, sir, it goes in the paint."

Daddy agreed to his secret method as long as it didn't make his truck drunk.

Let's get back to my story.

I believe Pop could drive anything he got in; he had been driving house-moving pull trucks for decades at this point of his life. Pop knew this truck inside and out. I already knew the first things to do – check the oil and check your tires. Then, we start the truck so it can build up air pressure for the air brakes.

Pop said, "I know you are familiar with the gears, but I think the first thing you need to learn is how to snort around."

And I knew what he meant. Sitting in the driver's seat with my hands on the wheel, I thought to myself, *Does life get any better than this?*

Inspirational words from a teenager, right?

Pop said, "Let's start off by learning to snort around the yard for a little bit before we hit the road."

I just smiled. All I could do was smile and say, “Yes, sir.”

We start off with the main transmission down in “Grannie,” or first gear, auxiliary in first gear, and the brown lipe in first gear. I knew he was expecting me to go through all four gears on the auxiliary and brown lipe, then shift the main transmission from first to second, and run through the auxiliary and brown lipe gears.

But my favorite part of driving this truck, “the snorting around,” came with the proverbial catch – if I so much as missed one gear, I would have to pull over, put everything back down in the “low hole,” and start over. Grinding gears was not acceptable.

Every time I messed up and ended up grinding the gears, as we call it, Pop would snicker to himself and say, “I’ll take a half of pound of ground meat for supper please.”

I think he got a lot of pleasure out of telling me, “You missed a gear. Pull over and start over.”

My response was always, “Yes, sir,” but I assure you, I was sure hoping and praying the loud diesel engine covered my mumbling of frustration under my breath.

Then, his next words were, “Donna just fiddle with them sticks until you get it right.”

I guess he had to make that statement to me so often that it went from “fiddle with them sticks” to just “fiddle sticks” as he pointed to the gear shifts, while laughing the whole time.

Oh, yes, he thought he was being so funny. Me, on the other hand, didn’t think it was funny at all. Didn’t matter what he said, I knew what he meant.

And yes, I had to stop and start over a few times… well, maybe it was several. Okay, it was a lot of times. Pop kept saying practice makes perfect, keep fiddling with them sticks, you’ll get the hang of it. Pop was right, and after a few days it started becoming easier and easier. I was so excited. I was like a tight pair of jeans, ready to bust wide open.

We had driven around the house-moving yard after work for a few days, so Pop said, “Let’s get out on the street.”

As we were about to pull out of the yard and onto the street, it decided to start sprinkling. Sitting there in silence, after a few minutes, it went from sprinkling to full-on pouring. Guess the frown on my face said it all.

Pop looked at the rain pouring down and looked over at me and said, "Well, the way I look at it, you must be able to drive on wet streets as well as dry streets."

My frown quickly turned into a smile, big as Texas. I responded by telling him, "I can drive a car and a pickup. I *will* learn to drive this truck."

Pop said, "I believe you will, Donna, I believe you will. Just remember, this truck is a lot heavier than a car or a pickup, and it will not stop on a dime."

Well, that tidbit of information got my attention. Never thought about that, nope, never even thought about the weight of the truck. That first lesson in the rain sticks in my mind, even today.

Pop said, "Pay attention to all sides of your truck."

After my first "hands on" street driving lesson, I changed my mind. It is very different! You literally find a rhythm between the gear shifting and clutch – almost like poetry in motion.

This revelation from Pop gave me a whole new understanding of big trucks. So much to learn, but I was not about to give up. No, sir, not giving up, no matter what. Pop not only taught me everything I knew, but also he taught me everything he knew. For that, I will always be grateful.

By the time my "official" lessons were over, I could "snort" around in the truck, swapping gears, without grinding or making "hamburger meat." Something that tickles me still today. It's been a while since I have driven this truck, but you know what they say – it's like riding a bicycle. It'll come back to you.

I can still hear his voice. His words are forever etched in my heart: "You done good. I am proud of you."

Each and every person on God's green earth really wants to hear those words. They lift us up and give us the courage to go on to the next project with a "can-do" attitude. Thank you, Pop, for everything. I am grateful you made me stop and start over until I got it right.

Now that I have told you about my driving lessons with Pop, who had the patience of Job (the man in the Bible) teaching me how to drive a very complex truck, I figured it was appropriate to give you a little background on this man. Daddy told me this story back when I was still in grade school.

Papaw Snow and Daddy were working on a job over in the Weatherford area when the local Sheriff pulled up on the job site. He shut his squad car off, got out, and started walking straight to my Papaw.

"C.A.!" the Sheriff was hollering over the big pull truck engine. "C.A., you got a minute?"

Papaw stopped what he was doing and walked over to the Sheriff. After exchanging the usual good morning pleasantries and the joke about getting a house-moving permit before pulling out on the road, the Sheriff said he had a proposition for him.

Well, Daddy said that when he heard that, he stopped and got down out of the pull truck.

"Okay," Papaw Snow said. "What's on your mind, Sheriff?"

"C.A., I have a man in the back seat of my squad car. He's in some trouble and on his way to jail. As I was driving by your job site, I remembered you telling me you could use some good strong men to work in your crew. Are you still looking for help, sir?"

"Well, yes, I am."

"Then, I think I have someone you may want to meet. If you agree to hire him, then I will let him work out his troubles. If not, then he goes to jail on a state-paid vacation."

Papaw asked the Sheriff to get the man out so he can look him over. Daddy said the handcuffed man literally unfolded out of the backseat of the squad car. He was a large, muscled-up man that looked like he was not afraid of hard work. After the Sheriff made the introductions, Papaw walked up closer so he could ask the man some questions.

"Are you afraid of work?" No, sir, was the answer.

"Do you intend on stealing from me?" No, sir, was the answer.

"Will you give me a fair day's work for a fair day's wages?" Yes, sir, was the answer.

"Will you show up for work every day?" Yes, sir, was the answer.

"Do you know anything about house moving?" No, sir, was the answer.

To which Papaw responded, "Good, that way you don't have any bad habits for me to break. We will teach you the right way from the beginning. Okay, Sheriff, take the cuffs off of him. He is hired."

Papaw started walking back to the job when he stopped and turned around to the Sheriff and his new hire. "Oh, yes, Sheriff, if he doesn't keep up his end of the bargain, I will—"

But before Papaw could finish his sentence, the Sheriff interrupted him and said, "C.A., if he doesn't keep his end of the bargain, just call me and I will come get him."

With the look of a serious poker player, Papaw looked the Sheriff straight in the eye and said, "I will, sir. I will call you and let you know where the body is."

Needless to say, there was a look of horror on not only my Daddy's face, but also the Sheriff's face and Papaw's new hire. And that is how Pop came to work for the house-moving company.

So many times, we say "work for," but it didn't take long before it became "work with." It seems Pop had found where he fit in. Everyone was happy with the arrangement.

This young man, Tommy, worked not only for my Papaw Snow, but he also continued his house-moving career up to his retirement with my Daddy, before he passed away.

All of us Snow grandkids knew him as "Pop." It wasn't until I went to work for Daddy and started doing payroll that I learned his real name.

I knew him as Pop, I knew him as Tommy, I knew him as a mentor and friend.

**Lesson learned:** *The way I see it, there are two possible lessons learned in this "saying." You pick which one works for you. Tommy proved second chances can be a wonderful thing, if you aren't afraid of hard work.*

*Or you can interpret it as when you hear someone grinding gears and you want to mess with them, just holler out, "I'll take a pound of ground meat please!"*

*P. S. Last year I learned that there is an actual instrument called fiddlesticks. I saw it with my own eyes and heard it played... really amazing.*

# Running around like a chicken with its head cut off...

Several of us were sitting around at Grannie's house on a rather warm summer afternoon. It was Sunday.

Seemed everyone was letting their belt out a notch from all the delicious food we had just eaten. Homemade chicken and cornbread dressing, yeast rolls, green beans, black eyed peas, mashed potatoes, potato salad, corn on the cob, tomato and onion salad, sliced tomatoes, onions, and pickles – all grown on the farm. Man, you talk about putting on the feed bag. My Grannie and Grandma sure could!

If you got there early enough, you would get to go down to the garden with them and help gather the vegetables for lunch. Grannie would make sure I had not only one of her aprons on, but also a bonnet. The first time I saw Grannie and understood she was wearing an apron, I asked why she wore one all the time.

She explained to me that aprons and bonnets are very important. An apron will protect your dress (Grannie only wore dresses) from getting dirty whether you're dusting the furniture, mopping the floor, feeding the livestock, tending to the chickens, gathering eggs, milking, or cooking. Then, if you forget your basket, you can fold the bottom part of your apron upwards and carry anything, like eggs, wood for the stove, or vegetables.

But aprons are also used to wipe away tears or even sweat from your face. If your hands get wet from the garden hose or water troughs, you can dry your hands on your apron. Then, if company comes calling, you take off your apron and your dress is still nice and clean, and by wearing your bonnet outside, your hair is never windblown, and your skin is not sunburned.

When I say bonnet, I mean like the ones they wore in the 1800s. They were all homemade with really cute feed-sack material. The first time I remember putting on both an apron and a bonnet, Grandma told me I looked like "Sun Bonnet Sue."

I asked, "Grandma, is she one of my cousins?"

She laughed and said, "No, it's an old quilt pattern."

But that's enough about aprons and bonnets. Let's get back to the food... specifically the desserts.

Oh, my goodness, the desserts – homemade banana pudding (like you cook on the stove and not instant pudding), caramel nut pie, butter pound cake, coconut crème pie, sweet potato salad, her famous "nasty cake," and all the brewed-on-the-stove sweet tea you wanted. And yes, we still use all her recipes to this day.

Grannie and Grandma were sitting on the side porch, sipping their tea by the orange trumpet vines, talking and laughing periodically. I had been in the kitchen with Mother and others helping wash dishes and put things up after everyone was finished eating. Something very special, at least to me, was that if you helped cook or clean, you wore an apron.

Grannie's apron had to be wrapped around me almost twice, but I didn't care; it was my Grannie's. As I finished the chores assigned to me, I took off my apron and hung it on the back of the kitchen door where Grannie would hang hers using a step stool as I was not quite tall enough to reach the hook. Then I set out to find Grannie and Grandma. While I was walking out of the kitchen, through the dining room and into the living room, I felt the slight afternoon breeze on my face, and it felt good.

To explain a little bit, Grannie and Granddad didn't have central heat and air – only a small swamp cooler, and it was only used when it was absolutely necessary. So, most of the time during pretty weather, they had the windows and doors open with the air flowing through the house. Fresh country air flowing through; nice, very nice. Grandma had always told me that opening up all the windows and doors in a house was healthy for us. It aired it out, cleaned out any unwanted odors, and made everything feel fresh and clean. Walking through Grannie's house, I watched the curtains dancing in the breeze. Much simpler times, and to be honest, I miss those days. Nowadays, most people are afraid to open their homes like they used to do. Really sad, isn't it?

Anyway, as I walked out to the porch, Grannie and Grandma were almost in tears laughing. I stood there and asked what was so funny. Grandma was the one who composed herself first and began telling me the story:

"Many years ago, when your mother was about your age (8 years old), she overheard a phone conversation between me and my mother, your Grannie, about our menu for our upcoming Easter family meal.

"Usually what we do is make all the desserts the day before, so that on the day of the family get-together, we only have to worry about preparing the meal. So, I went over to my mother's house, met your Great Aunt Tommie there, and we each started working on a dessert. Your Grannie's shotgun kitchen was long and narrow, so sometimes, when several of us were in there trying to cook and bumping into each other, we would holler out, 'Is this a three-butt or four-butt kitchen?'

"We didn't care. We were laughing and having so much fun, kinda making a mess all at the same time, when out of nowhere we heard a blood curdling scream. I immediately knew it was your mother, and we all dropped what we were doing and ran for the screen door. As we ran out the side porch door, we were just in time to see your mother running down from the barn and screaming at the top of her lungs, being chased by a chicken whose neck had been stretched out so long it was dragging the ground. Your Grannie hollered, 'That hen's running around like a chicken with its head cut off!'

"Seems your mother had decided to imitate what she saw your Grannie do and tried to wring the chicken's neck. Since she didn't have the strength in her little arms to do the job in a quick manner, the more she rung the neck, the more it stretched out. The whole time, the chicken was fighting her, squawking, and trying to get away. Evidently, your mother got tired and dropped the disoriented chicken to the ground. She thought the chicken was chasing her, and that prompted her to scream and run.

"I ran after your mother, and your Grannie ran after Sunday's lunch!"

**Lesson learned:** *Sometimes it's best to leave the neck-wringing to the professionals.*

# You think I look bad? You should see the other guy.

Sonny, my main roping horse, was all saddled and standing in the stall waiting for our time to go rope. His bridle and tie-down were hanging on the horn of the saddle, ready to go. Staying tied up by his water bucket helped assure he did not dehydrate in the record heat Arkansas was having. My roping partner and I had been practicing every week. We saved up our money for the entry fees working towards this event for over three months.

Well, it was getting close to our time to rope, so I decided to go ahead and put his headstall and tie-down on and head over to the warmup pen. There are those that said Sonny was a little on the "fluffy" side, but I say he was just pleasingly plump. And he didn't get that way from not cleaning his feed bin when fed. Sonny was reaching down for that last bite of hay, and I was reaching down to put his head gear on, and just as he got that last bite, he raised his head back up and *bam!* We clashed – his head to my right eye.

I reached up and didn't feel any blood, so I figured, *Well, it was a long way from my heart. I'm good.* Even though I could feel the swelling starting, I decided to keep going. I had driven too far and paid my entry fees. I wasn't about to let my roping partner down; nothing was gonna stop me now.

My roping partner and I backed in the roping boxes. That's when her husband started giving her all sorts of instruction to the point that she was getting very nervous. Her horse had not been "facing" very good lately. The more instructions he gave her to do, the more frustrated and nervous she was becoming, and all of those nerves were transferring right down to her horse.

Let me explain myself a little bit here. We had been practicing our tail ends off for months, put up $150.00 per person (that's $300.00 per team) in entry fees, and drove all the way from Fort Worth, Texas to Fort Smith, Arkansas.

There were a lot more male teams roping than female at this time, so being a woman in a predominantly male sport, there was more to prove. The stands were packed full of onlookers, and the temperature, along with the humidity, was horrid! When you look at the whole picture, it was enough to make you beyond nervous.

Finally, I had enough of it. I raised my voice, hollering out loud, "Look at me!"

Well, when I said that, everyone within 20 feet stopped and turned around and looked at me.

I told my partner, "You go out there and rope the snot out of this steer. Then you better get a deep seat and a faraway look and hold on, because I'm gonna get me two feet, and when this big red horse stops, he will sling you and your horse around. Nice clean run and, ta-da, facing problem solved."

(If you are not familiar with roping terminology, you may want to look it up.)

I truly think my little outburst helped, as she appeared to have snapped out of it. I gave her a smile, and she smiled back. We were ready. In no less than five seconds, she nodded her head, calling for the steer.

Even though we had a great run, and her horse did face, we didn't win any money. When things don't go my way, Daddy always told me to try and find at least one positive outcome. And here it is – man, did we look good running down the arena!

Seems my eye had started swelling up, and it was getting more tender to the touch. After our run, we were walking our horses out the end of the pen when her husband walked up and saw my eye.

"Dang, Donna, what happened?"

I told him me and Sonny had a meeting of the minds. I lost, he won. Then, her husband made me go sit down out by their horse trailer, handed me a Ziplock baggy full of ice to put on it, and said to sit there and don't move.

I have to admit, the ice did help, so I sat there a while, listening the whole time to my stomach growling. Getting my horse ready to rope and with all the excitement, I had completely forgot to eat breakfast and was beyond hungry. Looking around with my one eye that wasn't swollen shut, I didn't see my friends, so I decided to sneak over to the concession stand. Figured I could run over to the concession stand, get me some food, and get back before anyone knew I was gone. Yes, ma'am, good plan.

Standing in line, a couple of men looked at me and said, "Hey, lady, your eye and the side of your face looks bad. It's all swollen."

I kept a real straight face, looked them in the eye, and answered back, "You think this looks bad? You should see the other guy!"

**Lesson learned:** *Life's short. Give them something to talk about.*

# You heard me the first time. I didn't stutter.

It was a little past their curfew, so Daddy and Uncle Corky were, let's say, being extra quiet. Since their house sat on a corner, Daddy turned off the headlights as they rounded the corner to keep them from shining in their parents' bedroom. Uncle Corky opened the "glove box" on their car, pulled out the men's cologne, and they all but took a bath in it trying to conceal the evening's activity – smoking cigars.

As with most older homes, like they lived in, there were a lot of unusual moans and groans the house would make. The wooden back porch steps creaked, the back door hinges squeaked, the screen door creaks, and the wooden floors in the kitchen creak. So, trying to be extra quiet so that you could sneak in was not as easy as they thought it would be.

In order to get to their bedroom, they had to go through the corner of their parents' bedroom, so they decided to take off their shoes and see if that would help. Guess what? It didn't work. Evidently their mother was waiting up for them, sitting in the dark in their bedroom. Papaw Snow had already gone to bed.

Just as Daddy and Uncle Corky were tippy toeing, being as quiet as a mouse, they heard a very familiar voice: "Harold Don, Herschel Lloyd, stop right where you are!"

(Herschel Lloyd was Uncle Corky's real name.)

Now, picture this. Daddy is 6'2", Uncle Corky is 5'9", and they are completely paralyzed by a 5'1" woman. They stopped dead in their tracks and slowly turned around just as they were instructed to do.

First question she asked was why they were out past their curfew, to which they replied, "Mother, we are sorry. The time just got away from us."

She looked them in the eye and said, "Okay, I can see that happening."

Now, it was at this point that Daddy and Uncle Corky thought they were in the clear, so they quickly said, "We are sorry, Mother," and as they were turning around to head to their room, she said, "That's not all, boys."

She went on, "Harold Don, Herschel Lloyd, you know the rules. You have to give me a kiss on the cheek to say goodnight."

Daddy said, "Mother, you and Daddy must be so tired, so we're gonna go on to bed now."

As they were turning to head to their bedroom for the third time, it must have been the breaking point for her. That is when her body language changed, and her voice changed.

"Boys, you heard me the first time. I didn't stutter. Give me my kiss goodnight."

You have to understand that Grandma Snow handled business right where it happened. No calling Papaw Snow. Nope, she was a force to be reckoned with, and she didn't need any help from anyone.

Daddy told me his life flashed before his eyes, and he just knew he was going to see Jesus early. So, he stepped up and kissed her on the check with Uncle Corky following suit. They thought they had pulled the wool over her eyes by holding their breath while they kissed her on the cheek.

Next words out of her mouth were, "Breathe in my face."

Daddy was the first to speak up. "Oh, Mother, you taught us better than that. We just couldn't do that. That's bad manners."

Grandma Snow looked up at both of her sons and asked how many cigars they had smoked.

"Did you enjoy it? Are you gonna take up smoking now? Guess it doesn't matter what generation you were born in; teenage boys are all the same. They seem to think their parents are clueless, when in fact they are not."

With both of her sons standing there looking at her, realizing their plan had failed, Daddy was the first one to break. "To be honest, Mother, I threw up, and that is why we are late, and I have never been so sick to my stomach in all my life. And I promise you, I will never smoke a cigar or anything else the longest day I live."

I remember asking Grandma Snow about this incident, because I thought it was as funny as all get out. She said that no matter which one of her kids were out running around or on a date, she just couldn't go to sleep until she knew they were home safe. Her and Papaw had come up with this rule, "a kiss on the cheek goodnight," so she could tell if they had been drinking.

As a rule, the boys were in before curfew, so that night seemed a little odd to her. It had crossed her mind that maybe they'd had a few drinks, but she never suspected smoking. What she didn't tell her sons was this: their heavy cologne made it all the way into their bedroom about 30 seconds before they got to her doorway. When she smelled that, she figured it was smoking and not so much drinking.

And to his dying day, Daddy kept his promise to his mother.

**Lesson learned:** *News flash to all teenagers – your parents were once teenagers, too. You have not done anything they haven't tried to hide from their parents.*

# You complain, you do it...

One of Daddy's greatest pleasures was going hunting and fishing with his friends. Looking back, I can see where this was a great opportunity for him to get away from the rat race and just unwind from all his responsibilities at the business. Daddy worked so hard from sunup to way past sundown, out in the cold or hot weather, never complaining. Who knows, he may have needed a break from us kids as well.

About three weeks before they were scheduled to leave, Daddy started packing all his clothes and gear anticipating the day they pulled out heading to Colorado. Every night he would pull his list out and go over his "pile of gear" again and again. His hunting rifles were meticulously cleaned, several times, and ready. Sleeping bags were washed and ready, tent ready, hunting clothes washed and packed. Skinning knife sharpened, game bags and tags packed... Oh, yes, and bullets.

So, the weekend before Daddy and his hunting buddies were supposed to leave, they had a meeting to plan out the route they would drive, the snacks they needed on the road, the food they would take with them for camp, etc., etc., etc.

Kinda funny listening to them talk about the food. One of them suggested they take a lot of Spam. His reasoning was that if they didn't bag any game, they wouldn't starve. Everyone agreed on some rations just in case, but not all Spam. Some suggestions were jerky, homemade fried pies, potted meats, sandwich meat, eggs, and bacon. They lost me at potted meats. Yuck!

Then they had to decide who was doing what job. And it would appear, to this group of men, the most important job was that of the cook. I suggested the whole rock, paper, scissors thing, or everyone put their name in a hat and let someone draw out the first cook. But, instead of taking any of my suggestions, turns out, the other men had been hinting for Daddy to take the lead on this.

Daddy spoke up and said, "Okay I will do it. But the first person to complain about my cooking has to take over, then whoever complains next has to take over, and so on and so on."

Daddy gave one last glance at each man and said, "You complain, you do it."

After mulling it over, each man agreed to Daddy's terms, stating that was fair. When all the guys left, I asked why he caved in and agreed to be the first cook on the hunting trip. Daddy chuckled and said, "Have you had their cooking before?"

Shaking my head no, he said "I have."

Departure day was here, and they were all off at the crack of dawn, heading north. After a long road trip, they arrived at what would be their home away from home for the next 10 days. Once they set up camp, Daddy started setting up his kitchen and preparing the next meal. He had been hunting since he was a little boy with his Grandpa Thoma, and therefore, he knew a whole lot about camping, hunting, and living off the land. So, all the meals he fixed, everyone raved and raved as to how delicious it was. They were throwing compliments all over the place.

Over the next several days, Daddy finally got tired of being the only one who fixed the meals and was trying to come up with a way to make someone complain so they would have to take over the cooking. He tried scrambling the eggs real hard, but that didn't work. Burnt the friend potatoes, but that didn't work. Coffee was weak, but that didn't work. Left the bread opened up so it would get hard, but that didn't work. No one would complain, because none of them wanted to throw in the towel first and have to take over the cooking job. And then he had a brilliant idea, or so he thought.

He had some big homemade cookies left that Mother had made. So, he went out and gathered a few berries and a few other berry-looking items. Came back to camp, fixed a great supper, and watched as everyone just sat back with their bellies full. This is when he asked, "Could I interest anyone in dessert?"

Wow, dessert too? The men were pleasantly surprised. They were all saying, "Oh, yeah, bring it on."

He took the desserts he had made and set them in front of his hunting buddies. They were going on and on about how delicious it looked. Ted picked up his cookie, and it was almost to his mouth when Daddy hollered out, "STOP! I can't do it. Put your cookies down. There's a little extra "berry" I put in your cookie that is really moose droppings. And I just can't let y'all eat them. Sorry, guys."

While Daddy thought they would all be furious with him, they all busted out laughing. So, from that day on, it was decided that in order to be fair to everyone, maybe they should all pitch in and help with the cooking.

**Lesson learned:** *Before you eat anything, give it a good looking over and check for any funny looking dingle berries.*

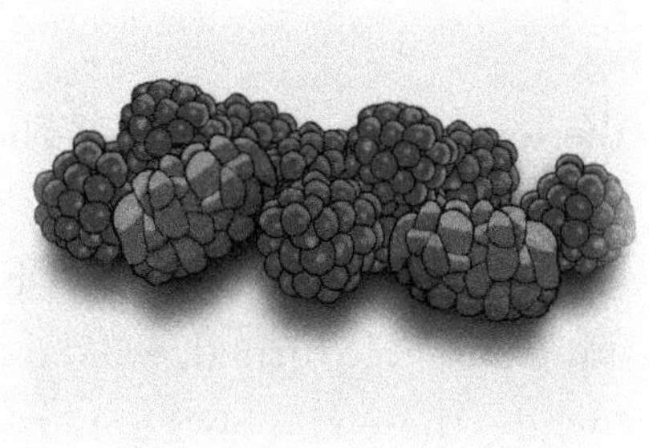

# You are so dead!

I was heading to the high school, as I had an appointment to meet with a counselor on behalf of a grandson that was living with me at the time. I was taught a long time ago that arriving five minutes ahead of schedule is right on time, so as usual I was a little bit early for my appointment. When I walked through the office door, immediately to my right was a wall of chairs with the receptionist area being at the back of the room. Even though it was a large area, it was an unusual configuration. I checked in, then sat down waiting for the counselor to see me.

After a couple of minutes, I heard the office door open. Looking in that direction, I saw a man come in with two young teenage boys in tow. He pointed to the seats over by me and told the boys to sit down. Through the snickering and open disrespect, they showed this man, whom I figured out later was a teacher. They eventually sat down about two seats away from me.

He walked up to the receptionist and said, "There they are, trouble with a capital T."

It was clear to me by the look on his face that he'd had all he could handle of these two young men. He turned, walked right back by us, and left the office. All the while, these two boys are just acting out all kinds of disrespect through physical motions and verbal insults.

I couldn't help myself, so I turned to the boys and said, "What are you guys in here for?"

They looked me over like, *Who are you?*

They said, "Well, they think they are gonna tell us what to do. Trying to make us do schoolwork and homework. Ha! We do what we want, when we want, any time we want, and can't nobody stop us! We have rights!"

My reply to them was, "Oh, I see."

One of them, who seemed to be the leader, said their teacher told them they were being handed over to some old woman who taught the "troubled kids." They also wanted me to know that they were going to give this old bat a run for her money. Of course, the thought going through my mind was that both of them needed their legs whipped. Evidently, they had never experienced their dad's belt clearing six loops in 2.6 seconds!

So, all three of us sat there, me waiting for the counselor and them waiting for the troubled kids' teacher.

In a few minutes, someone came in a side door by the receptionist, and for some odd reason, that voice sounded very familiar to me. Before I could turn my head to see who the woman was, I heard, "Donna Paulette!"

I grabbed the arms of the chair I was sitting in. My heart stopped. I could barely breathe, as I knew immediately whose voice it was. It was my Great Aunt Patsy Ruth!

While I do love my Great Aunt Patsy Ruth, you didn't mess with this woman. Oh, my gosh. This is the last person you wanted to make mad. While she was a fierce protector of her family, she was very strict. But she was also fair. And she didn't take no "lip" off of anyone, man nor beast! If you think I am exaggerating, ask her two sons. Trust me, they will back me up. The way I was raised, when an adult called your name, your response should be immediate and start with "yes, ma'am" or "yes, sir."

The two boys looked at me and said, "Hey, lady, are you okay? You look like you just saw a ghost."

Jumping up like the seat of my britches was on fire, I was walking quickly towards Aunt Patsy Ruth. With a little puzzled look on her face, she asked me what I was doing there. I told her about my meeting with a counselor for one of the grandkids. She hugged me, told me she loved me, and said she had to get back to work, that it looks like someone had delivered two boys to the office she was taking back to her class.

You know, I was born at night, but it wasn't last night. Suddenly everything was falling into place. The teacher bringing the two boys in, the two boys talking about some old woman that was gonna straighten them out, and then seeing Aunt Patsy Ruth. You see, since I grew up around Aunt Patsy Ruth, I knew her body language. I knew her tone of voice, and I also knew her disciplinary abilities. Right then and there, I believe I was having a flashback to my younger and dumber days of youth. Oh, man, better them two boys than me.

I hugged her neck, responding, "I love you too, Aunt Patsy Ruth," then started walking back to my seat. As I walked by the two boys, I looked at them and sat down. It was quite evident by the look on their faces that they were scared. With what I knew about the so-called "old, troubled kids' teacher," they needed to be scared. You can't tell me at that precise moment, they were wondering if they were gonna live to see tomorrow. They looked at me and asked, "Hey, lady, what should we do?"

To which I replied, "You had better do what she says when she says, and always speak to her using 'yes, ma'am' and 'no, ma'am.'"

As I turned to face them, in a trembling voice, I said, "If you don't follow my instructions, you are dead. You are so dead."

So, here came Aunt Patsy Ruth walking up. She called them by their names, to which they both jumped up as if standing at attention and hollered, "Yes, ma'am!"

Aunt Patsy Ruth winked at me, and I winked back. Hopefully, I saved their lives with my inside info.

**Lesson learned:** *Never forget that there is always someone older and smarter who can put you in your place faster than a minnow can swim a dipper!*

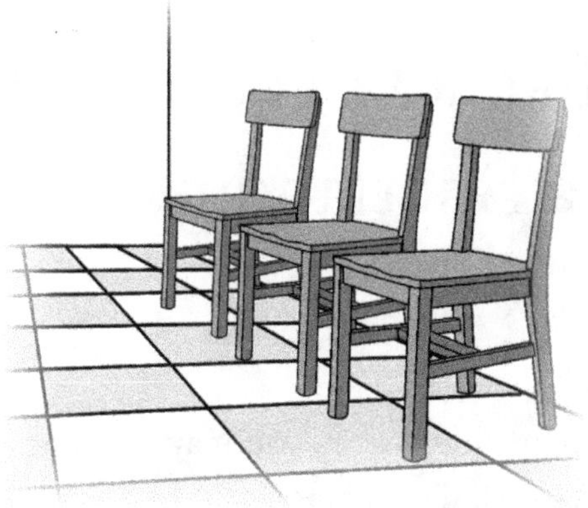

# Yep, like a tall cowgirl riding a Shetland pony...

Depending on how old you are, you may or may not have ever had the pleasure of laying down in bed sleeping on sheets that were so fresh from being hung out on a clothesline to dry. My great grandmother, my grandmother, and my mother all grew up like this, and while it was a lot of extra work, it was so worth it.

Now, these clotheslines were something everyone had in their backyards, and they were used almost every day but not always for hanging clothes on to dry. They did have more than one function. Not only were they used to hang clothes on for drying, but also they served as a tether line for a dog that wouldn't stay in the backyard. We even took sheets and hung them over the lines, making the most awesome forts you have ever seen.

They did, however, have one drawback. Over a period of time and after a lot of use, they begin to stretch out a little bit. Not as tight as when they were first put up, the lines began sagging.

If you lived anywhere near me, we played a lot of Cowboys and Indians or Sheriff and Bank Robbers. And if you were in the middle of chasing robbers, the last thing you needed was a clothesline that hung down too low. I am guessing by now you have figured it out as to what happened. Yep, it did, and I had the bravery mark to prove it for several days.

Most of the kids that I played with were my cousins, as there were not many kids my age on my street. They were mostly teenagers. This

Saturday afternoon found me, the Sheriff, and my deputies (which were my cousins) all hanging out at the "Saloon" (the doll house Daddy had built for us to play in) having a Sassafras to drink.

It was really a Dr. Pepper we had snuck out of the house when Mother wasn't looking, but we pretended like it was a Sassafras. Why Sassafras, you may ask? Well, we liked saying Sassafras better than Whiskey. Anyway, we heard someone screaming out that the bank is being robbed. So, me and my deputies ran out of the Saloon and saw the Robbers mounting up to ride off with all the town's money.

So, we jumped up on our horses that were tied up at the hitching post and started riding towards the bank. They may have been stick horses, but let me tell you, they could run like the wind. One of my deputies called out, "There they go!"

I was hollering, "Let's ride!"

The chase was on. We were determined to save the day, return the town's money back to the bank, and put the Robbers behind bars and throw away the keys. We were hot on their tail when out of nowhere, I got clotheslined. Turns out the Robbers had set a trap. They may have stopped me, but they didn't stop my deputies. Just a short distance down the road, my deputies overtook the robbers. Since our horses were faster than their horses, the deputies rode up beside each robber and jumped off their horse onto the robbers, knocking them to the ground. After a few karate chops, all the robbers were captured and handcuffed. My deputies came back and helped me get back on my horse, and we all went back to town. Justice prevailed! After we got back to town, I decided I had better go see the Doc.

So, I went running in the house crying like I was dying. Daddy was sitting in his chair and asked what happened, to which I replied, "I was chasing the robbers of the bank, and the clothesline knocked me off my horse."

Daddy said, "Your mother told me the clothesline needed tightened, as it was so low it would knock a tall cowgirl off her Shetland pony, and I guess she was right."

This "saying" brought to my mind something my mother and grandmothers did to us kids all the time. Bet yours did, too. Let me set up the scenario and see if you can guess what I'm talking about.

Picture this... You are a kid riding in the front seat of the car with your mother or grandmother, when suddenly either a stop light turns red or someone pulls out in front of you. What happens next? If you were riding in the front seat of the same car that I was, an arm suddenly appeared from your left and just about reached all the way over to the passenger door, thereby either knocking the wind out of you because it came across your chest, or you started gagging because it came across your throat. Either way, this with the "seatbelt" of the day. As we got older, we just called it getting clotheslined.

**Lesson learned:** *When chasing bank robbers, be prepared to duck!*

# What part of "no" don't you understand, the "N" or the "O"?

Back in high school, we had a class offered to the seniors that was called co-op. For those that don't know, it's where you basically go to school ½ day and work ½ day. I looked at it as preparing those of us not going to college for the work force after high school.

During my junior and senior year, I excelled in anything connected in "office" classes. These classes consisted of accounting, typing, shorthand, and basic office practices. I could take dictation and type the letter faster than a minner could swim a dipper. And that, my friend, is pretty doggone fast. So, for my senior year, I was qualified to take part in the co-op program with my real reason for enrolling in the program being to make some mad money!

Of course, I wasn't making but minimum wage back then, but as far as I was concerned, something was better than nothing, and I was setting the woods on fire. To give you a good laugh, minimum wage back in 1972 was a whopping $1.60 an hour.

The job I got that qualified under the co-op program only ran through the school year. So, when graduation came, I told Daddy I was ready to come into the family business full time. No more only working summers and weekends. I wanted to be a full-time employee, to which Daddy responded, "No."

My knee jerk reaction was, "Wait, what?"

To say I was shocked by his response was an understatement. Then it dawned on me, surely, I did not hear him right. As he was walking across the den heading to the kitchen, I called his name, and he stopped and turned around.

I looked him straight in the eyes and started laying out my defense, on the off chance that I didn't hear him right the first time. I have been learning from the best, and I knew I was a hard worker. Daddy stood there looking at me, and then his facial expression began turning to his "stern face," a look I really don't like seeing, and again tells me *no*.

Since that approach went over about like a candy bar in a public swimming pool, I began trying to present my case from another standpoint, and he abruptly stopped me with another *no*.

It was at this point I had used every trick in the book I could come up with to get him to agree to let me come to work for him. I just stood there, staring at him like a calf at a new gate. Daddy broke the silence, asking me, "What part of 'no' do you not understand? Is it the 'N' or the 'O'?"

I was definitely old enough and had plenty experience in my 17 years to know that tone of voice, that look, and decided it would be in my best interest to stop pressing the issue.

Then, as quickly as his stern face came, it left, turning into his soft smile as he saw I was backing off the "debate." He reminded me that I had graduated with honors in business. He felt it would be in my best interest to use my office skills instead of becoming a house-mover that consisted of long hours in the heat or cold, getting sweaty, dirty, and greasy. He looked at me and said, "Let's try it my way."

From past experience, I understood the best answer I could give him at that moment was, "Yes, sir!"

Since my brilliant idea of going to work for my Daddy had just been blown out of the water, now I had to find a way to get an office job. Several people suggested I go through a Temp Agency. So, I found one, made an appointment, and went in for an interview.

The interview consisted of taking a few "mock" telephone calls, alphabetizing files, taking a letter by shorthand dictation, and typing it up. After listening to what all they wanted me to do, I can remember thinking to myself, *I can do all of this standing on one foot!* Nothing hard about what they were asking me to do. The lady conducting the interview dictated the letter she wanted typed up. Then she took me in another room, that had a desk, typewriter, and typing paper, instructing me to take all the time I needed to type the dictated letter.

As I began putting the typing paper into the typewriter, I had the most uncomfortable feeling, like someone was watching me. After a few minutes, I pulled my letter out of the typewriter, turned around looking for the lady who gave me this task, and that's when it became clear where my uncomfortable feeling came from.

Just about everyone in this office was huddled in the doorway watching me type. Being a 17-year-old teenager, my first instinct was, *What did I do wrong?* I looked at the lady that had interviewed me and asked her if I was in trouble for something.

She explained to me it was quite the opposite. She went on to explain it had been a long time since they heard anyone type that fast. I handed her my letter and waited for her final conclusion. After a few minutes, she spoke up and said, "It is perfect, not one mistake."

Responding back to her, I asked, "Does this mean I get an A+?" That is how we were graded in my high school days.

She laughed at me and said, "I may not be able to give you an A+, but I can get you a good-paying job."

She had me at "good-paying job." Sending me with paperwork to an interview at a prominent business in Fort Worth, just on the west side of downtown, kinda made me feel like all those hours in class were finally paying off.

I have always been taught that five minutes ahead of schedule is right on time. So, I allowed myself plenty of time to drive to the interview, as I was hoping to make a good first impression. In case you are wondering, I did not wear blue jeans or work boots. Believe it or not, I owned a dress. Needless to say, the interview went very well, and I was hired on the spot. The job assigned to me was to be a personal secretary to one of the executive vice presidents.

Every day at lunch time, I would go to the break room to eat, like all the other secretaries. All the other secretaries didn't actually receive me with open arms, and I couldn't figure out why. It became apparent that if I wanted to find out the truth, a little bit of detective work was called for.

Turns out the position I was just hired for was the one they had all wanted to be promoted to. The opportunity presented itself for me to talk to the head of HR. So, I took advantage of this time and asked her what I could do to get on these ladies' good sides.

Her suggestion was to offer my help to them if they needed anything typed. "Since you can out-type anyone here, why not offer to help?"

When I went home from work that day, I told Mother and Daddy the dilemma I was facing and what the lady in HR suggested for me to do. Both were in agreeance with her advice. "But the flip side of that coin, Donna, is that helping someone out when you have the skill and talent to do it is good, but not to the point they are just using you. Just keep that in mind when making your decision."

At work the next morning, I went around to each of the ladies and offered my services, obviously hoping they would start treating me like one of the girls in the office, instead of an outsider. A few days later, it looked like my offer was breaking through the cold shoulder barriers. On my way back to my desk, I almost broke my arm patting myself on the back, thinking, *Good going, Donna, problem solved.*

With each passing week, when I came into the office, the stack of typing jobs increased. Sitting down at my desk, looking at the stacks of typing that needed to be done, I heard Mother and Daddy's words of counsel... to use your talents and skills to help is good, but not to the point where they are just using you.

Later that day, after I finished typing everything that had been put on my desk that morning, I returned the projects to each lady and politely told them, "No more." I had decided it was better to eat by myself than to be used.

Just like in all offices, there is a degree of drama, mostly centered around somebody sleeping with somebody. And yes, they are married, just not to each other.

Two or three days later, the head of HR said that the president wanted to see me. Off to his office I went with my pen and pad in hand. The door was standing open, so I politely knocked on the door, and he asked me to come in and have a seat.

In a very authoritative voice, he said, "I understand you have been causing trouble in the office."

I was in shock; this didn't make any sense. Surely, he had me mixed up with someone else, and trust me, I could name some names for him. Sadly, though, he didn't.

My response was, "I am being accused of causing trouble, sir."

I told him the only mistake I had made was trying to fit in where I really don't fit in. And if that wasn't enough "back-talking" to the head man, I kept on going.

"And the only problem here is that your girlfriend, to whom you are not married, is mad because I won't do her typing anymore. Because while I was doing her job, she was doing you!"

He just sat there staring at me, and I sat there staring at him. I was madder than a one-armed man in a paper hanging contest! When he finally gathered his wits and picked his jaw up off the floor, he stood up and leaned across his desk and said, "You should be fired."

That's when I realized I was standing up as well, with clenched fists, leaning over the desk and looking him square in the eyes. I said, quite loudly I might add, "Number one, you should be ashamed of yourself for having an affair with your secretary. Number two, you can't fire somebody that quit ten minutes ago."

This man was definitely at a loss for words, something I had not seen the whole time I had worked there.

On my heels, I turned and walked out of his office, holding my head up high. Went straight to my desk, gathered up all my belongings, and headed towards the back door and the employee parking lot.

As I passed HR, the faint round of applause stopped me dead in my tracks. I looked inside the room, and every one of the ladies in there was laughing and applauding. Seems like they had all wanted to see him told off but were afraid to say anything. They had to have their job.

All the way over to the house-moving office, I was putting together my speech to give to Daddy. When I walked in the front door of the office, there sat Grandma Snow, who was Daddy's secretary at the time. I asked where the job was that Daddy was on and if I could please have the address. So, from the office to the job site, I rehearsed my speech.

Well, I found the jobsite and got out of my little blue Jeep, walking around looking for Daddy. About that time, he came walking around the corner of the house, and I could tell he was shocked to see me on his job site and not at my office job.

He asked me, "What are you doing here?"

I said, "Daddy, we tried it your way. Now, we are gonna try it my way, because all I have ever wanted was to be a house-mover like you."

And the rest of the story, as they say, is history.

**Lesson learned:** *When Daddy tells you no two times or more, it may be in your best interest to just drop it. Unless you want to see how fast his belt can clear six belt loops.*

# Well, if this ain't a fine kettle of fish...

I will never forget the first time Mother and Daddy went on a hunting trip to Alaska and left me, fresh out of high school, in charge of Toni, Gary, and the house-moving company. I was seventeen, and Toni and Gary were still in school. Wow, that was a long, long, long time ago. That was so far back I think Moby Dick was still a minnow.

Daddy and I went over every job we had on the books. Everything I needed was in his briefcase – the drawings, notes, routes, permits needed, and which skids and dollies to use. I felt like I had made it to the big times. I was gonna go sit in the "boss's chair." In *his* chair, in *his* office! Excitement was setting in, but it only lasted for about 20 minutes. Carrying his heavy, and I mean *heavy*, briefcase, I marched straight into his office, set the briefcase down, and proceeded to sit down in his chair. And that is when it hit me... the weight of the job hit me.

I was carrying the weight that Daddy felt every minute of every day. It was very overwhelming to say the least. If anything went wrong, it was my responsibility. The "buck," as we call it, stopped with me. It's true, you never know the load someone else carries or what they go through until you walk a mile in their shoes.

So, as I sat there, taking it all in, something inside me started rising up. I kept hearing Daddy tell me to have faith in myself. He did. Since Daddy knows best, I decided that if he has that much faith in me, I should have faith in myself.

One of the most important things Daddy told me about moving houses was always go run the route yourself the day before you are set to move, just in case something has happened (lane closures, construction, accidents, etc.).

Well, I didn't, and that's where my problems began. The men decided not to tell me about a special maneuver they had been doing for years to get over a few sets of railroad tracks. A part of me thought that they didn't like the fact that a 17-year-old had been put in the driver's seat during Daddy and Mother's absence. Guess what? Donna was right!

Back in that time period, any house-moves around the city of Fort Worth required a "night haul" – on the roads after midnight and off the roads by 4 a.m. Staying up all night was not easy, but I definitely liked the less traffic aspect.

After refamiliarizing myself with the route written in Daddy's notes, we pulled off the lot at midnight. Everything looking good, following the route Daddy had written down, and all was going well. We turned on the service road that ran parallel with the interstate heading up to the next exit where we would be turning left to cross over the interstate on the bridge. I thought to myself, *This is all going smoothly, slicker than snot on a door knob.* That was, until I came upon a set of railroad tracks. I just stood there staring, kinda like a calf at a new gate. Out of my mouth came, "Well, if this ain't a fine kettle of fish," just like I had heard my Daddy say many times.

I turned to the men, who were all standing in front of the pull truck under the streetlight, and they were just staring at me, not a one of them saying a word. Each one of them had a little bit of a smirk on their face as if to say, "Now what ya gonna do?"

Their look said, "Looks like you're between a rock and a hard place... and we ain't saying a word."

Since it doesn't take me long to look at a hot horseshoe, I figured out rather quickly there was only one way out of this situation, and that was to back the house down the service road, get up on the Freeway for about a quarter of a mile (getting over the railroad tracks that ran beneath), and exit back off to my turn.

So, I said a quick little prayer, because at this point Donna needed all the help she could get, walked over to the Police Escorts, and told them my plan. Seemed the Police Officers picked up on what the crew had done and whispered in my ear, "We make this maneuver with your Dad all the time. It's the only way to get to that next exit. This time of night, there is little to no traffic on the interstate. All is good."

Walking over to the men, one of them spoke up and sarcastically said, "Now what?"

I smiled and told them, "Back the house up. We are getting on the freeway."

All their smiling smirks went down to a frown as they realized I had figured out what to do without their assistance. After about 30 minutes, we were back on the route heading for our final destination.

When Daddy called into the office on Monday morning to check on all of us and the business, he asked how the night haul went.

"Well, Daddy, I have to be honest with you. I didn't run the route out, and evidently the men weren't of the mind to tell me about y'all's 'special maneuver' to get over the railroad tracks."

His next words were, "Did you learn a lesson, Donna?"

To which I said, "Yes, sir, I did. I pulled an H.D. Snow on everyone! I remembered something you used to say all the time that you learned in the Military. Whenever you are faced with a challenge, improvise, adapt, and overcome. And maybe more importantly… I will never not run a route out again."

**Lesson learned:** *Note to self – always go check your route out before you put a 32-foot-wide house in the road in the middle of the night.*

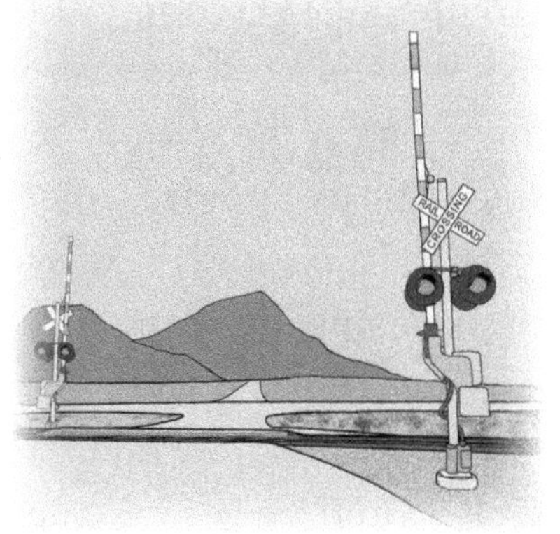

# Well, hug my neck...

Daddy and I were sitting down and eating lunch out on the job one summer day, enjoying everything Mother had packed for us – sandwiches, chips, homemade cookies, and Momma's sweet iced tea. Taking a few minutes to let our lunch settle before going back to work sure felt good.

I turned to Daddy and asked if we were gonna get to go to the rodeo coming to town, to which he replied, "Sounds like a lot of fun. Let's discuss with your mother tonight when we get in."

Now, I knew that Daddy had grown up around horses, livestock, and had tried his hand at calf roping, so I asked him what his favorite rodeo had been. Daddy sat there a moment as if collecting his thoughts and then laughed out loud and said there was one rodeo that he will never forget. So, I settled back, waiting for the story to begin.

After taking another drink of tea, I guess to wet his whistle, he said, "Donna, it had been advertised for weeks about the annual rodeo coming to town, and I had been given tickets by a man we had a moved a house for earlier in the week. If it wasn't for that man giving me tickets, we couldn't have afforded to go."

He continued, "I told your Papaw Snow I needed to get off early on the upcoming Saturday, as we were all going to the rodeo."

I spoke up and said, "You worked on Saturdays?"

"Yes, ma'am," he said. "You worked six days a week for your Papaw. Only day off we got was Sunday. Off to the rodeo we went – me, your

Mother, you, Gary, and a big diaper bag. Yes, this was before Toni was born. Our tickets were up in what we call the nosebleed section, but we didn't care. We were at the rodeo.

"Now your little brother, Gary, had a little habit that helped him fall asleep as a baby. He would take the end of the cloth diaper and rub it back and forth under his nose, and presto chango, he would fall asleep. The cutest thing you ever saw. Well, suffice it to say, at that stage of my life, I didn't think there was anything cute about my baby brother." Daddy went on to say that even as a toddler, he still kept doing it.

"Well, it was about his bedtime, so your mother gave him his cloth diaper to hold and waited for him to fall asleep. Then out of nowhere, and before me or your mother could react, he threw the diaper up in the air, and it caught some of the breeze and floated gently down a few rows in front of us and landed on the back of a man. A really big man, at that. Obviously, this man felt something on the back of his neck, reached around, and pulled it off. Seeing it was a diaper, he quickly held it between two fingers away from his body. I hollered down there and said, 'Sorry about that. It's a clean diaper that my son threw.'

"So, each row in front of us passed the diaper back, and no sooner than I handed it back to Gary, he threw it again, with me hollering, 'Well, hug my neck!' And guess who it landed on?"

I said, "The same man as before?"

Daddy just nodded yes. "And just like before, they handed it back up to me row by row.

"I guess in all the excitement and noises of the rodeo, Gary just couldn't fall asleep. Seems Gary had invented a game of, 'Let me throw my diaper and you fetch it, Daddy.' Gary started getting a little fussy, so your mother got a chocolate bar out of the diaper bag. That seem to settle him down, but, boy, was he messy. So, we were trying to clean him up and watch the rodeo all at the same time. About that time, the crowd started screaming, 'Hold on, hold on, hold on!' It was saddle bronc riding, and some guy was making a great ride.

"Well, we both stopped cleaning up the chocolate mess, looked up, and were joining in with cheering him on, not really paying attention to Gary. He reached up and pulled the diaper out of my hand and threw it again, and yes, it landed on the same man a few rows down. However, this time, when he pulled it off his neck, he quickly held it out in front of him. Seems he had a whole new respect for diapers, as the chocolate must have looked like something else to him.

"I said, 'Sir, it's only chocolate and nothing else, I promise. If you will please pass it up to me one more time, I assure you I will sit on it for the rest of the night.'"

Daddy started laughing thinking of this past event, and I was laughing listening to him talk about it.

"Well, lunch is over. Let's get back to work."

As I was putting my gloves back on, I stopped and asked, "Did the saddle bronc rider win? Did all the screams and cheers help him?"

Daddy said, "I don't recall, to be honest with you. I was too busy trying not to get killed by Godzilla over a chocolate-covered diaper."

**Lesson learned:** *Ask yourself this question, is it chocolate or not?*

# Well, Hell's bells...

Now, this story goes so far back in time that it was not mandatory for anyone to wear a seat belt. Most often on a Friday night, you would find several, if not all, of us eight grandchildren over at Grandma and Papaw Snow's house.

We all loved being together, and that was a time when your cousins were your first, and often times, best friends. But we also loved being there because we were with our grandparents. Us grandkids had come up with a very smart plan as to how we could all end up over there. And no, I'm not giving out any secrets.

Wait just a minute... It just dawned on me that this gave all our parents the weekend off. I am this many years old and just now realizing why our parents never said no when we asked, begged, or bargained if we could go over to Grandma and Papaw Snow's house. Seems like they must have had a plan as well; they wanted to get us out of their hair for the weekend. Hmmm, very sneaky.

Without fail on this Friday night, immediately following supper, Grandma Snow would start the, "It's time for everyone to take their baths and go to bed," speech. This in itself was a huge undertaking. Think about this – all eight of us kids waiting our turn for a bath, to brush our teeth, and get ready for bed using the one bathroom. As we stood in line down the hallway of their house, waiting our turn in the bathroom, it probably looked like a boarding house. Even after everyone was finally finished in the bathroom, none of us wanted to go to bed. We were all full of youthful energy, excitement for seeing each other, and the last thing on our minds was going to sleep.

As I sit here writing this, my mind is wandering back to those days. I realize memories are trickling from my eyes. Since one of my cousins passed away several years ago, any memory of my childhood is most precious to me. I hold them dear to my heart.

Grandma was hollering, "It's 9 o'clock! Everyone better get what part they don't want busted in bed!"

That was her way of saying, get in bed or get a whipping. When you don't want to go to bed, what's a kid to do? Well, you start asking for a drink of water, or the old "I have to go to the bathroom" trick. Each of us begging to *please let us stay up*.

After she'd had enough, she would say, "Okay, who wants to go first getting a whipping with Papaw's belt?" We knew she was at her breaking point. This was our sign; the games were over, and we'd better at least act like we were going to bed. The room went from loud like a playground to being as quiet as a mouse. Then the lights went out. Many times, as I peeked over to see Grandma's silhouette against the hall lights, I could faintly hear her say, "Good night. I love ya'll."

So, bright and early the next morning, after breakfast, we all loaded up in Grandma's car and headed out for the day. Some in the front seat, the rest of us in the back seat. Grocery store, drug store, barber shop, beauty salon, dry cleaners, etc., but the first stop was to go by the job and see Papaw Snow.

As we rounded the corner, we could see the big truck, the men walking around carrying cribbing blocks, house-moving beams, other equipment, and out front stood Papaw Snow. He was a very rigid and stern man, but when it came to his family, he was a gentle giant to us grandkids. Didn't matter where it was located – Grandma Snow always pulled onto the job site like she owned the place.

Once the car came to a complete stop and was put in park, she would get out and walk towards Papaw, while all of us grandkids were hanging out the window hollering out to him. He would come over and talk to us for a few minutes, then tell us he had to get back to work. Then his attention turned to Grandma Snow, with him handing her some money. So, Grandma would get back in the car, start it up, and put it in reverse. Oh, yes, by the way, Grandma Snow was very short, and it was not easy for her to see out of the car to back out, so Papaw would always help. Or should I say, he tried to help.

We all started giggling under our breath as we knew what was about to happen. It was the same thing that had happened over and over before.

Picture this – a very short woman trying to use her side mirrors and rear-view mirror, a husband who was trying to help her, and us grandkids giggling with Grandma fussing at us to be quiet so she could hear Papaw. Anybody watching this play out was getting quite a show. One thing was for sure – it was comical.

In order to be heard over the engine of the big truck, Papaw was raising his voice so that he could be heard. Therefore, Papaw was hollering at her, and Grandma was hollering back at him. He would say, "Thelma, listen to me, watch me!" Then he would start up again with his hand signals.

Just like many times before, when Papaw had reached the limits of his patience to the point of getting upset, he would say, "Thelma, I have to get back to work. I am standing back here, and I can see the street. You can't, so pay attention to my hand signals."

I really think all the directions Papaw Snow was telling her was going in one ear and out the other. She would stomp on the gas and then hit the brakes, stomp on the gas and hit the brakes, throwing us grandkids all over the front seat up against the dash as well as the backseat, throwing us in the floorboard.

Finally, Papaw would get fed up and holler out, "Thelma, don't stop until you hear glass shatter or smell $%&#!"

Grandma would slam on the brakes, lean out the car window, and yell back at him, "Carl, Carl, Carl! Well, Hell's bells, damn it, don't cuss in front of the grandkids!"

**Lesson learned:** *If Grandma Snow says it, it must be okay, right***?**

# Watching this is better than sex...

This hot day of filming found me and Toni at an auction over in the White Settlement area. In the middle of August, Texas is hot, so hot that even the bugs were staying in the shade. This house looked so bad from the outside with termite rot around the window seals. The roof was sagging like it was on the verge of caving in. The icing on the cake was the odor coming out of the windows; it was enough to knock a vulture off of a gut wagon, and I felt like I needed a Tetanus shot from just being near it.

In our line of work, we are always on the lookout for a house to save from the landfill. This house did not qualify. When I told Toni I would love to redecorate this house, she gave me a puzzled look. I looked at her and said, "Yes, ma'am, I would start with a 977 Caterpillar right in the front door. This house *needs* to go to the landfill!"

Anyway, Toni and I decided early on that we didn't want this house. However, that wasn't gonna stop us from running the bid up on anyone who acted like they wanted it. You may say, now, that's not very nice. To which I would reply, if they spend more money on this house, then maybe they won't have enough to go to the next auction, and we might have a better chance. You know what they say: all is fair in love and war and bidding on a house. Maybe I added in the bidding part.

So, when it was all said and done, we could tell that this other young couple really wanted the house. So, Toni and I helped them buy it at the highest price we could run it up to. Even Randy got in on the fun.

Well, suffice it to say, all of this was being filmed. The camera men, sound people, producers, and all of the flippers were literally melting into the ground. Well, during a break, I made a comment that was evidently overheard by the Field Producer that watching this young man try to move this house would be like going to the movies, and I would even bring popcorn to watch the show.

So, guess what happened? Well, this particular flipper decided he needed to straighten the house up, as it was "leaning a little bit to the north" (actually in this instance, it was leaning a whole lot to the north) before it was loaded on the dollies to move. About the time when he showed up with the house-moving equipment he had borrowed, Toni, Randy, and I showed up with lawn chairs and popcorn. We came to see a movie! And we knew it was gonna be a comedy!

Well, the camera men were filming, the sound men were recording, the producers were producing... and we were all sweating.

The Field Producer could tell everyone was just about done in, so she hollered over at me and said, "Donna, say something funny!"

I looked at her and said, "What? Like I can just say something funny on command."

But I knew what she meant. It had been a long day. Everyone was tired, hungry, and sweaty. So, I looked over at Toni and Randy and said, "Watching this is better than sex!"

Needless to say, even the Field Producer wasn't expecting this. One of the camera men literally dropped his camera, and everybody started laughing. I looked at the Field Producer and asked her if this was what she was looking for. Took everyone on set a few minutes to compose ourselves, but it was worth it. Sometimes you just need a good belly laugh.

Now, you are probably thinking the story ends here. Well, it doesn't. Have you ever just got caught up in a moment in time and never gave any thought to how it will be received in the future? Well... yeah, that happened to me.

So, we were at a watch party down at our local catfish restaurant. Everyone was eating and enjoying the fellowship, and we were on a countdown to the newest episode, which was to air at 8 p.m. Most people think Toni and I get to see the episodes before they air, but we don't. We are actually seeing it for the first time, too.

As we were watching the show, it never occurred to me that the Network would actually keep this footage as part of the episode. Guess what? They did!

As the show was playing out on the screen, we knew all the "behind the scenes" antics that took place. Toni, Randy, and I knew that particular part was coming up, and we were looking at each other and giggling to ourselves. We had the inside scoop! Inside joke, if you will.

As you may have figured out, there are usually what we call "cliff-hangers" scattered throughout the episode. They are strategically placed to make you want to come back after the commercial break. Well, here comes the scene, and guess what? There was the footage from filming with me that I thought would surely be left on the editor's floor. Well, it wasn't.

And just as soon as I said it, cliff-hanger! Everyone was laughing, and I was in shock. I was torn between being embarrassed, laughing, wondering what Mother and Daddy would say, or if I should just crawl under one of the tables. It was one of those hysterical moments in life.

Well, it seemed that the episode was a huge hit, and for that we are grateful.

But that's not where it all ended. A few weeks later on a Monday afternoon, we had visitors at the office. It was the Pastor and his wife. Now, this is the Pastor that we grew up with in Haltom City. He and his wife had retired from full-time Pastoral duties and were enjoying retirement.

They had decided to stop by on this trip into town to visit. Well, we all visited for a while, then he asked me how filming was going. It was almost like deja vu, a flash back to that hot day of filming.

I quickly asked, "Have y'all seen all the shows?"

To which Pastor replied, "Oh, yes, we wouldn't miss an episode."

Suddenly, I was transferred back to some of his "Hell fire and brimstone" sermons and knew what was most likely coming next.

So, in a very timid voice, I asked, "What about the episode where one of the non-house-mover flippers decided he could move a house?"

Pastor said, "Oh, yes, we saw that one too."

Was kinda hoping they had missed that part with a kitchen or bathroom break.

So, I said, "All of it?"

He replied, "Oh, yes, all of it."

He proceeded to tell us the evening's events. Well, they made sure they had supper early, and the kitchen all cleaned up. Settled in for the newest episode. After a short time watching the show, he heard a thud on the floor. It was his wife, who had passed out.

Well, when we all heard that, we gasped. Oh, my gosh! Not the Pastor's wife! I just knew I was headed straight for Hell.

I stood there waiting for the fire and brimstone to start falling. The voice inside my head was screaming, *Please say something... This silence is killing me.*

Then he started laughing and said, "It was really funny."

My heart started beating again, I finally started breathing, and quickly decided that maybe I'm not going straight to Hell.

**Lesson learned:** *Even pastors laugh.*

# Tonight's the night!

Grandmas are some of the greatest gifts we can have. If they live close by, they are usually very active in our lives. They babysit us, spoil us, run interference when we get in trouble, give us sweets when Mother says no and wasn't looking, let us stay up past our bedtime, and when they corrected us, it was never as hard as our parents. And they can be some of the best storytellers known to man.

Stories of a bygone era, many times about when they were growing up through all the good times and bad times. It just occurred to me; they are literally walking history books. Many times, as Grandma would be telling me a story, she would reach up and wipe a small tear while laughing all at the same time. The first time I saw that, I asked her if she was sad. Her reply was, "No, ma'am, not at all. Someday you will understand."

Call me crazy, but have you ever thought that you smelled their hand cream or perfume? That has happened to me many times over the years... and when it does, the memories come flooding back. Now, sometimes when I laugh, a tear comes out of my eye, too. I wish she was here so I could tell her that I do understand.

This is one of her favorite stories she used to share with me, and I remember this story as if Grandma Snow was sitting next to me at this very moment, telling it again.

As you can imagine, back in the early 1930s, there were some subjects you did not discuss openly. There were certain "words" that were only spoken inside your head, or if out loud, then only in a whisper. A prim and proper young lady knew what lines you didn't cross.

As a rule, each Sunday would find most families gathering after church for lunch and visiting. Oh, every now and then someone may have gotten a hot game of cards, or horseshoes, or even dominos going. But mostly, the family sat around visiting.

Sitting there on a Sunday afternoon after a family lunch sat my Great Grandmother Thoma in her favorite rocking chair on the front porch. Surrounded by her daughters enjoying the evening, men folk in the house talking, grandkids off playing chase. Crickets singing as the lightning bugs floated on the slight breeze that ruffled the hem of her dress. All was well in her world.

Evidently, my Grandma Snow and her sisters (my great aunts) had cooked up a little plan to try and catch their mother off guard and see if they could get her all flustered. So, picture this – an older lady, very prim and proper as a wife and mother, relaxing on the front porch with her four daughters, when out of nowhere one of them asks, "Momma, how often do you and Poppa have sex?"

Well, folks, I am here to tell you, the crickets stopped talking and the lightning bugs flew off when Great Grandma Thoma grabbed the arm rests on that rocking chair and brought it to a halt.

In her mind, she was saying to herself, "Y'all may be grown and married, but I can still put you in your place!"

With all the composure and grace she could muster, smiling as she leaned forward in her rocking chair, she said, "Well, girls, when your Poppa and I got married, many, many years ago, we decided to 'make whoopie' one night a week."

There was complete silence, as this was not the reaction her daughters were expecting. In fact, she was sure it was quite the opposite.

Then, out of the clear blue sky, and much to her daughters' surprise, she jumped up and hollered, "Tonight's the night!" She ran across the porch, threw open the front porch screen, and disappeared into the house, leaving her daughters in a total state of shock.

In my neck of the woods, that's what us Texas women call putting the shut to the up.

By the way, that subject was never brought up again.

**Lesson learned:** *Never try to pull a fast one on your mother. She's older, has more experience, and will probably leave you speechless!*

# Those two could take the pitchfork from the devil himself...

Do you remember when Toni and I were on the hit TV show, *Texas Flip N Move*? Not gonna lie – it was a lot of hard work, but we had a blast. Now, after losing both Mother and Daddy, it has become precious memories for all three of us kids. Some days, we would film for two hours, but as a rule, we filmed at least six to seven hours a day. Then, we had to go back to the office and take care of our regular jobs at the house-moving company. Can you say we needed more hours in the day? Boy, did we ever.

One morning, just as Toni and I walked in the backdoor to work, Daddy hollered for us to come to his office. So, we quickly set our stuff down, grabbed a pen and paper, and in we went. He wanted to tell us about an auction happening this very day over on the old Fort Worth Highway in Weatherford.

The house was one he had lived in along with his mother, dad, sister, and brother. Toni and I looked at each other, and at about the same time said, "All right, another auction."

Auctions were one of our favorite things to go do, especially if it was a good house and Randy was there bidding, too. Randy was an easy mark for me.

Turns out, this house was originally built by his grandfather, our great grandfather, many years ago. Then, when he was young, his dad (our grandfather) moved it. Many years later, our dad moved the house to where it was currently sitting. Therefore, if we were successful at the auction, this house would have been moved by three generations of Snows – Papaw Snow, H.D. Snow, and Donna, Gary, and Toni Snow. Wow!

Daddy looked us both straight in the eyes and said with a poker face, "Don't come back without that house."

That was all he had to say. During all this time, we were being filmed for the TV show, and the camera man was catching all of this on film. Daddy didn't have to say another word; we knew we were dismissed out on a mission.

Off to the auction we went, and guess who tried to win the house? That would be Randy. During the bidding, Randy kept bidding and bidding. We were starting to wonder if he was ever gonna give up.

He finally looked over our way and asked, "Just how do you plan to outbid me?"

I answered him back, "Because we have Daddy's checkbook."

Guess who won the house? That would be me and Toni. Yeah, Snow Sisters Texas! Toni and I could hardly wait to call Daddy and tell him.

When we got back to the office from the auction, we went straight into Daddy's office to fill him in on all the details of the day's events. He sat there smiling and laughing with us through it all, hanging on every word we spoke. Then, there was a peace that came over Daddy's face. I can't really explain it, but to me he appeared happy.

A couple of days later, Daddy and I went over to the house. I drove, as he was still recovering from knee surgery and had not been cleared to drive. No sooner did I get the truck in park, Daddy was trying to get out. I was hollering, "Hold on just a minute!"

Out of the truck he came with his handy dandy cane the Doctor was making him use. In reference to the cane, he didn't like it, not one little bit.

He stood there, looking the outside over, and pointed out to me the trim along the top of the house. It was so intricate. Come to find out, my Great Grandpa Thoma customed that work too. Such craftsmanship. When we walked in the front door of the house, it was if we had stepped through a portal back in time. In the midst of the silence, I realized the only footsteps I heard on the hard wood floors was mine. That is when I stopped and turned around to see my Daddy standing there smiling as he looked around the room. He pointed out where the television set, couch, and his dad's chair was all placed. Seemed it didn't matter that the room was empty; his memories and heart saw it.

Then he laughed out loud, and I turned around to ask what was so funny. I swear he was laughing through a few tears. He pointed down to what was once beautiful hardwood floors. "It was mine and your Uncle Corky's job to polish the floors."

I laughed and said, "Oh, you and Uncle Corky had to do housework?"

Daddy came up with a plan to not only polish the floors, but also keep their little sister occupied. So, their little sister, who was still in diapers, became the polishing tool they used. The floor was getting polished, and their sister was laughing as they pushed her around on the floor. It seemed like the work had been turned into play time. You just can't beat the old-time cloth diapers!

Turning and walking down the hallway, he pointed out which bedroom his sister was in and the other one him and Uncle Corky shared. When we walked into the kitchen, he looked at the kitchen cabinets from the left to the right and back again.

"Your Great Grandpa Thoma built these cabinets."

My response came out, "Wow! Daddy, they are beautiful and so unique."

He then stepped into what was his parents' bedroom. He pointed out the wall where their bed and dresser were and his mother's vanity, and then he pointed to a shelf and said, "That is where the only phone in the house was placed."

He remembered their old telephone number and even called it out. Wish I had written it down.

While Toni and I were working on another project, Daddy and Gary moved this very special house to the renovation yard. After a lot of hours, we got her all fixed up and shining brightly one more time, taking special precaution with the kitchen cabinets. Since the original bathroom sink was accidentally thrown out during demo, we needed a bathroom sink, and it needed to be of the same time period.

Modern and new were out of the question, and we knew exactly where to go. So, we set out for one of our favorite places that had any and everything you could ever want when it came to antique fixtures of any kind. We found what we thought would be a good fit, and it was at the right price. Problem solved... or so we thought.

One afternoon, as we were working on our final punch list and getting ready for auction day, Daddy stopped by to check on our progress. Truthfully, I think he just liked walking through this house of memories. Toni and I were quick to show him around. He was smiling and seemed really impressed with everything we had done... except the "pleased" look on his face and all compliments came to a screeching halt when he walked in the bathroom.

Honestly, I don't remember who spoke up first, me or Toni. One of us asked if there was a problem. This is when we realized he was standing in front of and eyeing the bathroom sink.

He turned and answered us with, "This is not the sink that came with the house."

We explained that the original sink was accidentally thrown out during demo, and when we went to get it out of the dumpster, it was broken by other building material scraps thrown on top of it.

He stood there, took a deep breath, and said, "Doesn't matter. This sink has got to go. Looks like someone painted it 'puke green.'"

Needless to say, we went and found another one, and yes, we got Daddy's seal of approval on it before it was installed. With his seal of approval, we were ready for auction. Auction day was two days away, and Mother Nature was having a fit. It rained and rained and rained. In my opinion, she was hormonal. Even though it had been raining and it was muddy all around the house, people came out for the auction.

Just as Myers Jackson (the auctioneer) was getting started and people started bidding, out of nowhere, Daddy walked right past me and Toni, heading straight for Myers. Before we could say a word, he told Myers, "There won't be any auction today."

He said he couldn't stand to part with the house. We were keeping it. Toni and I were smart enough not to argue with him. We were sure hoping Myers took our lead to not go against Daddy and keep quiet. We did, he did, and Daddy was happy. Ended up moving the house to some land that Toni and her husband owned.

Before we left the renovation yard that day, several of the Snow clan went back in the house and sat down. Daddy and his brother, our Uncle Corky, and a few of the cousins were there. To sit in one of the houses they grew up in, listening to them share their memories and funny stories, was like reliving it with them. What a blessing to share this moment in time.

When all the episodes aired, we had a "Watch Party" at a local restaurant with a bunch of people. It was so much fun. I guess this night, there were around 100 or more people there with us watching the newest episode. I am going to ask you to think back to when Daddy dismissed us out of his office that morning to go on over to the auction. Me or Toni never thought about the camera still rolling on him after we walked out.

Therefore, we had no idea what Daddy had said after we left, but we were about to find out. It was like he was talking to himself out loud and said, "Those two could take the pitchfork from the devil himself."

That quickly became a catch phrase that all the production company used when they saw us coming.

**Lesson learned:** *When you see two determined women going after something, you may want to stay out of their way. They could probably take the pitchfork from the devil himself.*

# They issue .45's at the door just to even the odds...

Over in the North Side of Fort Worth, there is a local little hole-in-the-wall steakhouse that boasted about one thing and one thing only – their chicken fried steak.

I learned from the owner of this fine establishment that their chicken fried steak had a "secret recipe." People would come from all over just to eat there. One night, the owner was checking in at each table, asking if everyone had enjoyed their meal, and every response including ours was, "It was over the moon delicious, and we were all singing the cook's praises."

I jokingly asked if he had that "special recipe" under lock and key somewhere. He laughed and said, "I wish." He went on to explain that when he first bought the place, it came with a provision – that he kept the lady that did all the cooking on the payroll.

"When I asked why I had to do that, the seller told me it was because she was the only one who knew the secret recipe." He laughed and said, "She calls it her job security. All kidding aside, she's a great lady and fun to work with."

However, this fine establishment didn't start out as a steakhouse. Its beginnings from decades earlier were, let's say, a bit more colorful. How do I describe what type of business this was prior to being a steakhouse? Here goes. Depending on what part of the country you are from, we here in Texas call it a "tonk" or even a "watering hole."

It was a place where the locals and Cowboys bringing in their herds to be sold in Fort Worth would "go and wet their whistle," which means having a beer or something stronger, having a friendly card game, or getting in a fight over a woman. Or if you are really bored, just get in a fight to have something to do. Yep, this place has been around for a long time.

After a long day of roping, one of my friends said, "Let's go check this place out I heard about. They are supposed to have the best chicken fried steaks in town."

Well, I jumped at the chance to not go home and cook. I was beyond tired, as was everyone else. Spending all day in a hot dusty arena really takes it out of you. So, it was unanimous; we were gonna go run a taste test on their chicken fried steak.

Seeing that we were all in agreement, I asked, "What's the name of the place?"

To which he said, "I don't know." Then I asked what the address was, and he said again, "I don't know."

Being a little frustrated at this point, I asked, "Then how do you think we are gonna find it?"

He said, "Well, they just gave me directions as to how to get there and what to watch for."

"Watch for? What do you mean, watch for?" This was getting crazier by the minute. I spoke up again and said, "Just tell us what they told you."

My lightning-fast mind said that since I am a house-mover by trade and familiar with just about every road in Fort Worth, I could at least figure what part of town this restaurant was located in. Anything to start narrowing down where this place was so we could go eat. We were hungry.

So, as he was telling us what he had been told, my mind was running the possible road maps in my mind. His directions consisted of, "Get off on Loop 820, go past the airport about five miles, and you will pass the motels you rent by the hour. Pass two pawns shops on the left, then you will come up to a red light. Make a right by the bank and follow that road for about a mile or two or three. Keep on the lookout for a fried chicken place on the left. If you see it, you went too far."

That's when I realized this restaurant was down near the old stockyards – not exactly a safe part of town. When I explained where this restaurant had to be, the two men spoke up and voiced their concerns about the location of the restaurant. The other girl and I looked at each other and grinned. Then I spoke up and said, "Don't worry, we won't let anyone hurt you."

So, with me in the lead, as I had a real good idea of where to go, off to the north side of Fort Worth we went.

We pulled into the small parking lot, practically taking all the space up with our horse trailers. Small parking lot, small building. *Hmm*, exactly how many tables can be in this place?

Standing there, giving the outside of the building a good looking over, I noticed it had a lot of neon signs on it with one window and one door. Yep, kinda scary looking. When we walked in, the lights were low, and you were immediately looking at a bar. The bartender was quick to greet us and ask how many was in our party, to which we replied there would be four.

The only way to follow the bartender was single file. By the time we reached our table, my eyes finally started adjusting to the low lights. Nice and cool inside, friendly people, a place to sit down that wasn't on a saddle, and a glass of cold iced tea. Life was good. The menu consisted of frog legs, calf fries, steaks, chicken fried steak, and bologna sandwiches. Everything seemed reasonably price – that is, with the exception of the bologna sandwich, and it was $99.00! I am telling you the truth; bologna sandwiches were $99.00.

We all told the waitress we wanted their famous chicken fried steak with all the trimmings. In a few minutes, we had a hand cut salad with their version of a homemade ranch dressing. Very cool and refreshing.

After they cleared our salad plates, out came the main meal – chicken fried steak smothered in homemade white gravy, with a huge baked potato and Texas toast. Man, was that food ever so good. What made this place so special was their recipe for chicken fried steak. You could order it with very light, medium, or heavy of their secret recipe.

Over on one side of the wall was an old jukebox, and it had all the old-time country and western tunes. I'm talking the ones you could actually dance to. People were feeding it quarters and picking songs. Lots of people were dancing around the room up and down the aisle between the tables. Deer heads, boar heads, cow heads, moose heads, and cow horns were the decorations on the walls. At Christmas, they went all out, draping garland between the horns and hanging ornaments on teeth. Very "Christmas-y."

So, where did the saying come from? Well, we must have all been very tired that night after roping all day in the heat, as none of us could remember the name of the restaurant. Therefore, whenever we all had a hankering to eat chicken fried steak, it became the place where they issued .45's at the door just to even the odds.

If you ever decide to try and find the place, know this. It's cash only. No credit or debit cards accepted.

**Lesson learned:** *Even though it may be a place that people tell you they issue .45's at the door just to even the odds, be careful not to judge a book by its cover. Oh, yeah, just in case you are wondering why it's a .45... they don't make a .46!*

# They done gone and lost their minds...

I was truly blessed growing up in a time when parents, grandparents, and even great grandparents felt it was their duty and took pride in teaching the youth of their family life skills.

While I can say I learned many things from all three generations, quilting is the one I am focusing on in this story. Through the years, quilts have grown to be priceless as they represent a lot of our past generations and ancestors. Many quilts tell a story, and some represent events. As a matter of fact, I have the very first quilt my Grandmother made all by herself, when she was getting married. The pattern is called a "Double Wedding Ring."

If you look at it close enough, you can see two wedding bands intertwined. Kinda romantic to me. She would tell me, "I hand-quilted it too tight," but I say it's perfect. It's perfect because she made it with her own two hands. Sometimes when I don't feel good or maybe a little sad, I go get that quilt and wrap it around me, and it almost feels like Grandma's arms around me telling me everything will be okay.

There came a time later in their lives when my great grandparents, Grannie and Granddad Graves, needed some "extra help" around the house. Aunt Tommie and Grandma decided they could kill two birds with one stone. By sewing for the public again, from Grannies house, they could be there for them and earn some "mad money" all at the same time. When you sew for the public, there is always left over fabric. Just about all their customers didn't care anything about the left-over fabric and gladly gave it to them. What do you do with all that left over fabric? You make quilts, of course.

Granddad Graves would walk by us on his way to or from the kitchen, look at the project we were working on, shake his head, and as he walked off, he would say, "You cut up fabric just to turn around and sew it back together. You women folk don't make a lick of sense to me."

Grandma had a keen eye for picking all the right pieces to put together for a quilt top. Watching her work her magic, it didn't take long for me to ask her if she would teach me to quilt. To which she quickly replied, she sure would. Now, one thing I will tell you about her – and to be honest, I do the same thing to this day – is that if you do it wrong, you have to tear it out and start over. And needless to say, in the beginning, I did a lot of tearing out.

My very first "official" quilt was a pattern called "Fence Rail." And I had put together what I thought would be the best colors from the pile of leftover material scraps. Grandma agreed. Grandma said I needed to do a lap quilt, as it would be a smaller project for me.

I asked why, and she said it was so I would not get discouraged. "Sometimes when you jump on a new project, and it is big, you can get discouraged. Most times, when you get discouraged, you never finish what you started."

After thinking about what she said, I had to admit she did have a point.

With scissors in our hands, we set to work cutting out all the pieces for my lap quilt. Sitting there looking at the pieces, I looked over at Grandma and proudly announced, "I'm gonna do this the old-fashioned way... by hand."

To which I thought she would be proud. Boy, was I wrong.

She looked at me and just shook her head and replied, "Why do you youngins want to make everything so hard?"

Then she explained to me that she herself had sewn many things by hand or on a treadle machine, not because she wanted to, but because she had to. She shared with me her memories of the day when they first came out with electric sewing machines, and how that was the cat's meow.

There I went and did it again – got away from the topic of my story. I will try to not do that again. Said I would try, no promises.

Anyway, a few quilts later, Grandma introduced me to "tac quilting." So, I took blue jeans from Daddy, Gary, Toni, and myself. Then I got pants from both of my Grand Daddies. I made what is called an "Improved Nine Patch" quilt. Got fleece for the backing, took old electric blankets, pulled the filaments out of them, and used that for the middle of my "quilt sandwich." This way, I knew the quilt would be warm. Then I took one block from each quilt and had it embroidered with a special note on it – one for Daddy, Gary, Toni, and keeping one for myself. These lap quilts would represent three generations of our family. After a few weekends, all three quilt tops were pieced and ready to be tac quilted.

As it turned out, we had all decided to go down to the lake for the weekend, and it just so happened that my floor quilting frames were there too. We joked that we could fish through the day and quilt at night.

So, we laid out the bottom fleece, set the electric blanket next, and finally, just like a cherry on top, we set the pieced quilt top in place. Once that was done, we attached each end to the frames, rolled it up, and started tac quilting. We had been quilting for about an hour, and I believe it was Grandma that said we had better check to make sure everything is still smooth on the underneath side of our quilt. Trust me, I have learned to check my work as I go along, because I did not want to have to tear any more out than was absolutely necessary.

Anyway, Grandma thought she felt a wrinkle, so we decided to stop and check our work.

Now, my quilting frame sits slightly lower than a kitchen table, making it easy to reach across the quilt. So, the first thing we did was bend over, and that didn't work. Cutting off our oxygen, that was kinda funny in itself. If you think I'm making this stuff up, you sit down in a kitchen table chair, bend over, and look up under the table. Only took us a hot minute to realize this wasn't working.

So, the obvious answer to us was get down on the floor, which me and Grandma did. Scooting up under the quilting frames and looking at our work from the bottom side, we immediately saw where our mistake was, and thankfully we didn't have to tear out too much. So, we started giggling about it.

About that time, Daddy decided to make a run on the kitchen for a snack during the commercials. He heard giggling and glanced over in our direction. All he could see was legs sticking out from under the quilting frames. He hollered at us, "What are y'all doing?"

We were already giggling, and this made us laugh even more. Then we heard him exclaim, "You women folk have done gone and lost your minds!"

My first quilt, the fence rail, led to many other firsts, not only for me but others as well. This quilt allowed me to share with others – some in my family and some not – the skill of quilting. We laughed, cried, tore out mistakes, and started over. But the best part was we pieced memories together that will never be forgotten.

**Lesson learned:** *Never pass up a chance to "piece together a memory." They are priceless.*

# There ain't no sense getting your tail end over the fence...

Many a weekend as a family, we went to the lake house so Daddy could get away from the telephone. Daddy loved to fish. Actually, he grew up fishing, so fishing and hunting became his escape from work. He was so dead set on having a quiet and relaxing time down at the lake house that he wouldn't even let a telephone line be brought in on the property.

Many a day would find us with a bucket of worms and a cane pole headed for the stock tank or the little inlets on the lake. We would bait our hook with a worm, throw it in the water, and see how many perch we could catch. After our can was full, we would go bait the trot lines. Side note – while perch are good for catching catfish, you still can't beat Great Grandpa Thoma's stink bait. That is, if you can keep from throwing up while putting it on the trot line.

For a while there, it looked like we caught more alligator gar than anything. The first time I saw one, I said, "That is not a catfish."

Daddy said, "No, it's a gar." More specifically, it is called an alligator gar, and when I realized the alligator gar was keeping us from catching catfish, I put it on my top ten enemy list.

For those of y'all not from around my neck of the woods, an alligator gar looks like a cross between an alligator and a prehistoric fish, with a long snout full of very sharp teeth. In other words, they are ugly but considered unique and native to Texas. These things have been known to grow upwards of 7 feet and can weigh about 100 lbs.

(Telling you this story reminds me of helping Daddy build trot lines – sweet memories I wouldn't trade for anything. Enough for memory lane right now, though. Back to the story.)

And for whatever reason, you can't go gar gigging until after dark. Daddy would light up the Coleman Lantern, gather our gigging poles that look a whole lot like a small version of a trident, and off we would go. It was like being on an adventure with Daddy. We were setting out to rid the world of alligator gar!

Daddy was so good at making fun of most anything. We all got in the Jeep – Daddy, Gary, Toni, and me. Mother didn't really care for going gigging. Said she would stay at the house and clean the supper dishes.

Now, understand, there are no streetlights, and while it is mostly pitch-black outside, tonight there was a full moon. Don't know how often you go to the lake or a river, but when the sun goes down, everything seems to change. Maybe it's just our imagination playing tricks on us, or maybe not. All I know is it's a lot scarier at night down by the water's edge. The waves slapping up on the shore, twigs breaking in the surrounding trees... makes you think a water monster is coming after you. But when Daddy is there, there is no fear because we are safe.

Anyway, on this night's adventure, with the help of a full moon, we pushed off from shore in the John Boat headed to first check our trot lines, then on to giggin' for gar. Daddy has been on this lake for so many years; he knows every curve and tree out there, which is a good thing for us.

To gig for gar, you have to go up in some of the narrow channels that feed the lake. As you approach the channel, you have to turn off the outboard motor and let the boat glide. Daddy would get out his oar and start guiding the boat up to where he wanted to go. Within a few seconds, you could see that the water was getting shallow.

Now, Daddy had two Coleman lanterns going, one at the back of the boat where he sat and one up towards the nose of the boat. You have to get a visual of where everyone was sitting. Daddy was at the back of the boat, me and Toni were side by side in the middle, and Gary was sitting at the nose of the boat.

The engine was off and pulled up so the rutter wouldn't drag the bottom of the channel. The only sound you could hear was the gentle swishing of the water as Daddy rowed the boat further up into the shallow water. I don't think me, Gary, or Toni were even breathing. We were doing some important work, getting rid of the catfish thieves!

Daddy said, "Now, start watching under the boat and listen for something to break the water." So, we sat there in silence waiting.

Then, out of nowhere, something bumped the bottom of the boat. We all froze, and then it happened again. Daddy whispered to us, "Don't move, sit still, and be quiet."

And sure enough, out from under that boat came the biggest alligator gar I had ever seen in my life. Well, okay, it was the first gar I had ever seen in my life. Wait a minute – that does qualify as the biggest alligator gar I had ever seen in my life. So far, that is.

Daddy had already schooled us on how to "gig" the gar. We were all set and waiting, somewhat patiently... Well, okay, not patient at all. With his lantern in hand, he raised it up to help light the area, moving it from side to side to see which way the gar was going.

When finally, his long nose came into view, and it seemed to be angling towards the nose of the boat toward Gary. Daddy hollered, "Now!"

All three of us started stabbing the water, trying to get the gar. Since the gar was closer to Gary, his stab hit first. And when it did, the fight was on, and I mean *it was on*! That gar went to fighting. Water was flying everywhere, the lanterns were sliding around, and all three of us kids were screaming.

Before Gary could get a better grip on his giggin' pole, that gar had started thrashing all over the place. He had to have been 6 feet long. Okay, well, maybe 5 feet. Oh, okay... He was around 4 feet long. But in the heat of the moment, he was huge!

Well, during the fight, Gary was trying to bring the gar up out of the water. Daddy was hollering, "Not yet, not yet!"

Gary couldn't hear him over me and Toni screaming. So, the gar was breaking water, and the water was going all over the closest person, which happened to be me. And I swear, I don't know what happened, but something just came over me. In the heat of the moment, I thought Gary was doing all of this on purpose. And that's when it happened.

I picked up my giggin' pole with every intention of knocking Gary plum out of the boat, and I was looking forward to hollering, "Man overboard!"

Daddy had a "backrow" seat and was taking everything in. He had to; he was the only adult there. Well, just as I was swinging my pole back so I would have good momentum, Daddy grabbed it and said to me, "Donna, there ain't no sense getting your tail end over the fence."

So, Gary didn't end up in the water, and he successfully got the gar. The only satisfaction I got was that Gary was completely drenched from fighting with the gar instead of me knocking him in the water.

Daddy gave me a real good talking to about getting all the facts before acting on a whelm.

There's no telling how many gars we got that night. Such memories that we three kids have experienced with Daddy. I think everyone should go giggin' for gar at least one time in their life.

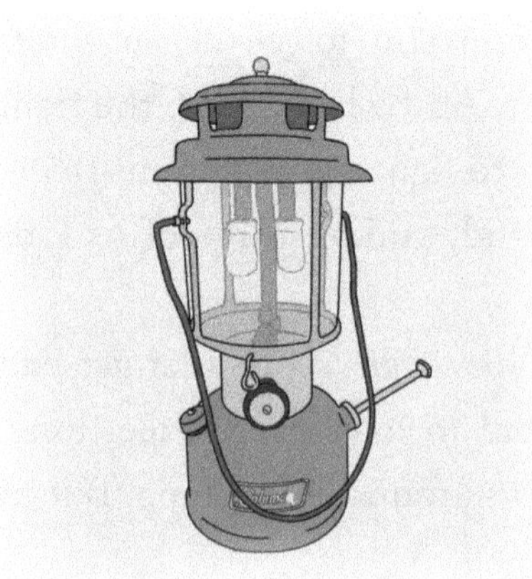

**Lesson learned:** *Just because someone does something to you, please don't jump to conclusions. Get all the information first, because there's no sense getting your tail end over the fence.*

# The only time I got to sit down was on the toilet...

A dear friend of mine, Karen, and I took Grandma Gandee up to see her sister-in-law, my great Aunt Tommie who lived in Tennessee at the time.

Aunt Tommie was so excited for us to come visiting and said we had picked the perfect weekend. It was square dancing weekend up in Finger, Tennessee, at the old gymnasium. I was quick to tell Aunt Tommie that square dancing wasn't exactly our thing, but we would love to go with them and watch.

She said, "Wait a minute. I remember back when you were in high school, you had a P.E. class that included square dancing, isn't that right?"

"Wow, you have a great memory for something that happened so many years ago," I told her. "And that's the problem here, Aunt Tommie. That was years ago, and I don't think I can remember any of what I learned."

That wasn't cutting it with Aunt Tommie. She gave me and Karen the talk about if someone comes up and asks you to dance, you dance. We kept saying, "Aunt Tommie, we don't square dance. We are here to watch."

She got a stern look on her face and said, "If someone comes up and asks you to dance, you better get up and dance."

And almost in unison, we both said, "Yes, ma'am."

Uncle Mansel was driving, and Aunt Tommie was doing all the talking as we were driving to the square dance. She was giving us the

"411" on the upcoming evening's events. To be honest, none of it was making any sense to me or Karen.

However, when we got there, it all started making a lot of sense. On one side of the gym sitting in the old wooden bleachers – remember, the dance was being held at an old gymnasium – was little, old, gray-haired ladies all dolled up. Hair all stacked up high on their head (you know what they say – the taller the hair, the closer to Heaven), big ole sparkly earrings, make-up, long and polished fingernails, and their dresses... Oh, my gosh, they were dressed "to the nines," as we say in my neck of the woods.

On the other side were little old men looking very dapper with their hair slicked back, shined shoes, some wearing "galluses" (otherwise known as "suspenders," which I learned from Daddy), and at least one whole bottle of cologne per man. We figured this was their version of "all dressed up." As Karen and I were looking around, we realized no one was wearing square dancing outfits. I asked Aunt Tommie, "I thought this was a square dance?"

She smiled and said, "That's what they call it. I never said that's what they did."

Karen and I were perfectly happy sitting there watching; it was kinda like a school dance back in high school. It was so cute, watching the little old men go ask the little old ladies to dance. I told Karen this might be a better evening than what we thought.

Out of nowhere, one man came up and asked me to dance, and Aunt Tommie's warning flashed through my mind, so I stood up, smiled, and said, "I would love to."

As we walked out on the dance floor, he smiled and told me he wasn't like all the other men there; he had all his own teeth. They were real. Just what are you supposed to say to that, I ask you?

My mouth engaged before my brain did, and I said, "That's wonderful, how nice for you." I immediately thought to myself, *Donna, you should have smiled and kept your mouth shut!*

You also have to ask yourself in these situations, how close to your dancing partner do you want to get? Ugh! Since most of them were shorter than me, in this situation, my height was to my advantage, especially if they had bad breath.

The unwritten rule of going dancing is this: if you are alone, meaning not with a date, most guys will send one guy up to ask you to dance. If you dance with him, they know you will dance. However, if you turn him down, no one else will come up and ask. Now, this is the "unwritten rule" in Texas, but it turns out, Tennessee uses the same rule.

Thus, Karen and I danced the night away with all the little old men lining up to dance with us. No sooner did one dance end that our escort would walk us back to where we were sitting, and the next little man was waiting for his turn to whirl us around the dance floor. Karen leaned over to me and whispered in my ear, "I thought this was a square dance?"

I just shrugged my shoulders.

With me and Karen dancing the night away, guess who wasn't dancing very much? All the little old ladies, that's who. Every chance they got, they showed us their displeasure that we were invading their "turf."

By the end of the evening, we both had sweat pouring off our faces and down our backs. Aunt Tommie came over and said, "You girls looked exhausted," and asked if we had sat down at all.

To which I replied, "The only time either one of us sat down was on the toilet! That's where we went to hide!"

**Lesson learned:** *If you get tired of dancing, go hide in the bathroom.*

# That's enough to knock a vulture off a gut wagon...

With all of us working together, we finally finished loading everything in the camper, which meant it was time to head out. Daddy called out to all us kids, "This camper will be leaving in five minutes. All aboard! And if you can't get aboard, get a shingle!"

Then he would start laughing. Daddy always made things interesting and fun. But he was serious – if you weren't in the bus, the bus just might leave without you.

Everyone – Mother, Daddy, Gary, Toni, and me – was all loaded and ready to go. We were headed out to the river in a homemade camper. Now, this camper was in fact the very first bus we ever had. We gutted and turned it into our own personal camper. It was painted blue and white, and just like everything else Daddy owned, it had a name – "Hunter's Paradise," painted on the side of it.

Now, this camper had a dual purpose – one as a family camper, and another as a camper for hunting trips.

On this occasion, the bus was the official family camper headed down to the river. We would be meeting up with others for a family weekend. One of the others I am talking about is my Great Grandpa Thoma, Daddy's Grandpa on his mother's side. Couldn't miss his rig; it was a bright yellow school bus.

Grandpa Thoma was a big man of German descent, who could literally build anything, fix anything, and fabricate anything. All these traits he passed on to his sons, grandsons, nephews, and anybody else who wanted to learn.

Hunter's Paradise was completely homemade on the inside – a coach, which also served as a bed for Gary and bunk beds in the back. The bottom bunk was for Mother and Daddy, the top bunk for me and Toni. It had a little all-in-one commode and shower. In hindsight, there are those that would indeed call it "rough," but we only saw it as something we had made with our own hands. The best part, though, was we would get to go places, like weekend trips to the river and possibly a summer vacation.

Well, this happened to be one of those weekend outings – camping on the river. We loaded groceries from the house that Mother had cooked and baked. We would be camping down on the riverbank, and that was free. We were in some tall cotton!

The main point to this story is really all about my Great Grandpa Thoma. Now, all of us great grandkids just called him Grandpa Thoma. Remember I told you about his camper, the yellow bus? Well, the interior design was almost identical to the one in our bus. Guess I know where Daddy got his idea, right?

Grandpa Thoma was known for his ability to catch the biggest and tastiest catfish the river had. I had asked Daddy if there was a secret regarding where to fish. Daddy laughed and said no.

So, my next question was, "Is there a special fishing pole or special trot line material?"

Daddy laughed and said, "No, wrong again."

I looked at Daddy and said, "Well, then, I guess I don't understand. How in the Sam hill do you and Grandpa Thoma always seem to catch the best catfish?"

Daddy said, "This is something that really can't be explained. It's something you to have to see with your own eyes and smell with your own nose."

I stood there looking at Daddy like a calf at a new gate, uttering the only thing I could think to say: "Huh?"

He went on to say that Grandpa used homemade stink bait. I remember thinking that was an awful name for something that caught some of the most delicious catfish you ever slapped a lip over.

Daddy motioned for me to follow him, which I did. As we walked, he asked, "Have you ever wondered why we park so far away and always upwind from Grandpa?"

"I guess I never thought about it. Just figured you were getting the best level parking place since we are on the side of the riverbank." Then I realized we were walking a big circle, approaching Grandpa's bus. To say this was getting a little weird is an understatement.

We walked up to his campsite, and I could see that the front door, as well as the backdoor, was open. Daddy hollered as we approached the bus, "Grandpa!"

To which you heard, "Come on in, Harold."

So, Daddy and I stepped inside Grandpa's bus.

The instant I stepped into the front of that bus, my eyes started watering and my nose tried to jump off my face. "Oh, my gosh! What is that horrible smell?"

Grandpa Thoma looked up from his cutting board and said, "Little one, that is the best stink bait ever made, guaranteed to catch the tastiest fish around."

I looked at Daddy, who was tearing up too, and said, "I can't stand it any longer. I think I'm gonna throw up."

And I ran down the steps of the bus and out the front door. All I heard was laughing from Daddy and Grandpa. Daddy followed me out of the bus to make sure I was okay. Through my tears, I could see Daddy trying not to laugh as he approached me. I was literally speechless.

"What in the world is that stuff?"

Daddy was laughing so hard he could hardly speak. Finally composing himself, he said, "It's a special recipe of Grandpa's called stink bait. And while it can knock a vulture off a gut wagon, there is nothing better around to catch fish with."

That was the first and last time I ever got that close to Grandpa Thoma's bus. It don't take me long to look at a hot horseshoe, as they say, so I made sure that all future camping trips, I'd remember Daddy's lesson about staying up wind.

**Lesson learned:** *They say curiosity killed the cat; in this case, it may have been Great Grandpa's stink bait.*

# That sounds about as good as a dying calf in a hailstorm...

Several years ago, a few of us took our campers and went down to the first Monday at Canton, Texas, which we all loved to do. You never knew what treasure you might find there. Everything from antiques to tools. For me, the fun was finding a treasure and then trying to negotiate the best deal with the seller. Come to think of it, the negotiating was the most fun of all.

On a previous trip to Canton, I was looking for a quilting frame. I was wanting one that stood on the floor and not one that was designed to drop down from the ceiling. So, I told Daddy to keep his eye peeled for one, and that I had $50.00 to spend. Later that afternoon, I ran into Mother and Daddy riding around on the little scooters you can rent down there. Mother said, "It sure beats walking all over the place."

Well, Daddy said he had a surprise for me and motioned for me to follow him. After about 20 minutes of walking, we stopped at a booth. And guess what? They were selling quilting frames just like I had wanted. They were so pretty and well-built, too. I was jumping up and down with excitement, that is until I saw the price tag – $100.00.

Daddy spoke up and said, "I thought we could be partners on these quilting frames."

I looked up at him and said, "Partners?" I figured I could trust Daddy, so I agreed to be partners with him.

Daddy said, "Let me handle the money. Give me your $50.00."

I handed him my money. He turned to the man and gave him a $100.00 bill, then turned back around to me and handed me $50.00 and said, "There's your change."

While I was standing there trying to figure out Daddy's math, he asked the man if he happened to have a permanent marker pen. The man said he'd go look.

In a few minutes, he came back with one and handed it to Daddy. The man spoke up and said, "What are you going to do with the marker?"

Daddy answered him back and said, "I'm gonna write on these here quilting frames."

"Write on them?" the man said in an elevated voice.

Daddy said, "I paid for them, which means I can do anything I want with them."

And he did. He wrote, "H.D. Snow and Donna Snow – partners." That is how I got my quilting frames, made $50.00, and I still use them to this day. Now that I ran down this rabbit trail, let's get back to the story at hand, shall we?

Anyway, while it was rather chilly at night, the weather was perfect during the day for walking around and shopping. As usual, when I go camping, I carry my instruments with me. After a fun but tiring day of shopping, we would all head back to our campers, fix something to eat, and just relax and enjoy each other's company. Usually, we would all bring food out of our campers to a common area and set up a buffet; sit; eat good, home-cooked food; and visit. However, as the evening went on, the night air was getting a little chill to it.

Daddy spoke up and said, "Hey, let's all go in my camper," where it was a little warmer, and he asked me and my friend to entertain them. A friend of mine, who happened to be at Canton that weekend as well, had brought her guitar down, and I had my banjo. So, we went back in my camper, got our instruments out, and decided to warm up a little bit. We picked out a few songs, put our little "impromptu" show together, and next door we went.

When we walked into Daddy's camper, they had set up three chairs for us out in the middle, and they all sat in a half circle around us. Look at us – we had a stage.

When I looked over at the third chair, there was a single red solo cup. Guess Daddy could tell I was perplexed by the cup and offered up an answer. Come to find out, it was for tips. Of course, the first thought I had was, "Oh, boy, more money to spend on treasures tomorrow!"

So, in an effort to make a lot of money that night, we decided to really put on a good show… and we thought we had.

I have to be honest with you, this impromptu show was a blast. With each song we sang and played, one by one they would get up and walk over to the solo cup and put a quarter in.

Quarters! Quarters! We were hoping for $1's, $5's, $10's, $20's, or $100's. But, hey, we were grateful for the quarters. They spend, too. Seems like the total take that night was $5.50, and we split it down the middle. We made $2.25 each, setting the woods on fire with our first paid gig.

After the performance was over, I couldn't help but ask Daddy if they really enjoyed our performance, to which he replied, "Y'all sounded great, right up there with a dying calf in a hailstorm."

**Lesson learned:** *If you ever get a chance to perform, do it, even if it's just for quarters. And if you ever get a chance to watch a performance, be sure to tip well even if they do sound like a dying calf in a hailstorm.*

# That's like putting lipstick on a pig...

Randy had asked me and Toni to come look at a project he was working on. Knowing Randy the way we do, we knew something was up. We arrived at the address he gave us, and there he stood grinning like a possum eating persimmons. Yeppers, instantly we knew to stay on our toes.

So, Toni and I got out of the truck, looking around, and I guess the confused looks on our faces gave it away. Randy quickly walked over to us and said he had a brainstorm and came up with an idea and was wanting to know what we thought about it.

I asked him, "Are you sure it was a brainstorm, or could it have been a cranial flatulation?" (Fancy words for brain fart.)

Toni hit me on the arm and gave me one of those looks like Mother used to give us. Basically, the look was, "Say it again, just say it again. You won't like the outcome." So, we looked at each other and reluctantly agreed to look at his project. Randy seemed really pumped up about this project; he was grinning from ear to ear like the cat that ate the canary.

As we were walking with Randy around some buildings, he was really building his secret project up. Finally, he stopped and said, "Well, what do you think?"

To which we both looked at each other and said, "What do we think about what?"

Randy was holding his arms out towards what appeared to be a room that had been cut off a garage. Now, Toni and I aren't the type to bust someone's bubble, but standing there staring at a piece of a room that was kinda leaning a little, it was hard to hide our immediate reaction.

While I do have the unbelievable skill of holding my tongue, that skill set evidently does not transfer to my face. Randy said, "Now, hold on before you draw any conclusions."

I said, "Okay, you're right. I will hold my verdict for after your presentation. Fair enough?"

He said, "Yes, ma'am, fair enough."

So, Randy began explaining his plans to turn this into a tiny house. Since tiny houses had become huge sellers about this time, he came up with the brilliant idea to have one or two to offer for sale along with regular-sized houses.

I spoke up and said, "Kinda like a test program?"

Randy smiled and said, "Exactly!"

"Okay, Randy, I like you're thinking so far. Continue."

Randy went on to describe all his thoughts and ideas. With this structure having a taller roof line, it gave the interior more of a roomy feel, and it didn't make you feel cloister phobic.

Toni and I stood there listening intently to every word he said.

Randy said, "Picture a loft on this end of the building. Something simple, not real fancy, thereby keeping the costs down. Since the loft area is limited on height, how about an area big enough to put up to a queen size mattress on the floor, with a window to see out? You can put containers up here to hold your clothes. Under the loft area will be the kitchen and bathroom. That way, I can put the plumbing for the kitchen sink on one side of the wall and the bathroom plumbing on the other side. Still working out how to lay out the bathroom area, as it will only have a shower – no tub."

Randy walked back towards the area we had originally walked in. "This is where the living room / eating area will be. Really leaning towards a wood laminate floor and not carpet."

After he was through laying out his plan, we could tell he was waiting on our final judgement. Toni and I both offered our ideas for consideration. His face lit up and said, "Oh, my gosh, yes! That's what I needed was input from y'all. Your ideas are great, and I'm gonna use them."

Really good use of the square footage was my final take on his project.

Now, I can't speak for Toni, but let me tell you about my personal opinion of Randy's idea. I looked him straight in the eye and said, "Randy your idea is awesome! In fact, it's not only awesome, but also flipping brilliant! Love the idea of taking a small square footage building and making it into an overgrown playhouse with all the luxuries you can put in it, yet keeping the costs down so it is very affordable and attractive to prospective buyers. And you make a profit all at the same time."

As soon as I completed my last sentence, Randy responded by rearing back and sticking his thumbs in the suspenders of his trademark overalls, grinning from ear to ear. Speaking up, he said, "I thought you would like it."

"Oh, yes, I love the idea. However, if you use this little piece of junk building, it would be like putting lipstick on a pig."

**Lesson learned:** *It's still a pig, and not all pigs look good with lipstick. Ha!*

# Spit it out, just spit it out...

I think we have all said this saying at one time or another when we saw someone at a loss for words or just trying to get the right words to come out. But I have to say, the very first time I heard it was from Daddy. After that, this saying took on a whole new meaning. To fully lay out this story, let's take a short trip down memory lane, shall we?

Do you remember when you first got your driver's license, and you would get excited to go run errands for your parents? Your mother would say something like, "Oh, no, we are so low on milk and bread," then you would literally jump over furniture running towards her, hollering, "No problem, Mom. I can run to the store for you."

After a few weeks of this, it dawned on you that your Mother never really went to the store anymore. Then shortly after that is when you realized you had inadvertently become the chauffeur and errand-runner, and that's when the newness wears off. Daddy told me about when he first got his driver's license. He would gladly run all the errands that his Mother and Daddy would send him on. This was clearly the time before all the newness wore off for him. Yes, I remember those days, do you?

Back to my story...

On this particular day, Papaw Snow was about to send both his sons, H.D. and Corky, on an errand. Grandma Snow was in the middle of spring cleaning in the middle of summer, so everyone was working around the house and cleaning out the garage. By the time they finished, the whole back end on the pickup was filled up and ready to be taken to the dump. Quickly tying everything down securely, Daddy and Uncle Corky were more than glad to take the trash down to the dump, because they knew that when they were done unloading the trash, they could go cruising on the streets in Weatherford.

Out of curiosity, I asked Daddy what their definition of "cruising" was.

He said, "First off, your truck or car had to be spotless and shiny. Make sure you had on a clean shirt and good-smelling cologne with your hair slicked back. Then, you go cruise on into town down to the malt shop, pull into a spot, place your order, wait for the cute 'hop' to bring your food, but more importantly, you had to act cool. As a matter of fact, this was the malt shop where I had my first part time job."

I said, "Wait a minute. I thought the only job you ever had was being a house-mover?"

Daddy laughed and said, "Well, I didn't last long at the malt shop. You see, I was a 'soda jerk.'"

I laughed out loud and said, "You were a what?"

Daddy looked at me and said, "Being a soda jerk had its perks. Like waiting on all the cute girls, and the best part was all the free ice cream you could eat."

I asked him what made him leave that "cool" job as I was giggling.

He said he dropped a whole crate of glass cups used for sundaes, and they shattered. Oops! Yep, I can see why he didn't stay there very long. Oh, my gosh, I did it again. I got off topic. Back to the story.

Just as they were pulling out of the driveway, Papaw Snow hollered at them, "Tell Hoofas that I have some work for him, and bring him back with you!"

Talk about taking the wind out of their sails. Their plan to go cruising around town just got shot down and would have to wait for another day. Off to the dump they went. Daddy and Uncle Corky pulled into the dump, unloaded the trash out of the back of the pickup, swept the bed of the truck out, then headed over to where Hoofas lived.

It wasn't very far, because he literally lived at the dump. Now, Hoofas' living conditions were a bit less than normal. His house was a tent under a big tree. This was a warmer time of year, which meant that Hoofas slept outside, unless it was raining, by his tent on a cot. If you couldn't see Hoofas, you surely could hear him, because he snored loud enough for a deaf man to hear him, kinda like a runaway chain saw.

As Daddy puts it, "Hoofas could snore a cord of wood an hour."

As they walked up to Hoofas' tent, there he was, sleeping on his cot, mouth wide open with flies going in and out. Daddy said standing there watching the flies going in and out of Hoofas' mouth just about made him and Corky feel like they could throw up.

Since there were many stories going around about where Hoofas came from, they had learned a long time ago not to startle him. They tried making enough noise walking up, but to no avail. They started poking at each other, saying, "Go wake him up."

"Not me, you go wake him up."

Uncle Corky came up with a plan to flip a coin to see who would be the one to put their life on the line to wake up Hoofas. He took a coin out of his pocket, looked at Daddy, and said, "Heads I win, tails you lose."

Up in the air the coin went, and it came right back down with Corky shouting, "I won, I won!"

So, Daddy walked up to the end of the cot by Hoofas' feet and started kicking the end of the bed, trying to wake him up. A startled Hoofas began in the middle of a snore, sucking wind in with a lot of flies. Hoofas was trying to wake up, sit up, and spit out flies all at the same time.

While he was trying to say something to Daddy and Uncle Corky, all he could do was spit out flies. They could tell he wasn't very happy they woke him up. Daddy and Uncle Corky thought this was too funny and started laughing.

Daddy said, "Spit it out, Hoofas, just spit it out. You're amongst friends. Daddy sent us up here to get you, said to tell you he has work that needs to be done."

Seemed his large belly made it a chore for him to fully sit up. He finally caught his breath after getting all the flies out of his mouth, licked his fingers, and attempted to slick back his hair. He grabbed his jacket, and without so much as uttering a single word, went and got in the bed of the pickup and sat down.

"I looked over at your Uncle Corky and said, 'Well, I guess this means he's ready to go.' We were really glad Hoofas chose to ride in the back of the pickup, because we knew there was no way he had a shower in that tent where he lived. In other words, he stunk!"

When they pulled into the driveway at the house, Papaw walked up and told him about the work he had for him to do. As Hoofas smiled, Daddy and Corky saw a fly between his two front teeth. They both quickly turned and walked off, because they knew that if they laughed at him, even if it was Hoofas, that would be considered disrespecting an elder, and they would be in bad trouble with their Daddy.

Something about his story puzzled me for a while, so I went back and asked Daddy for some clarification.

"When you got to the part about Uncle Corky flipping a coin to see who would wake Hoofas up, you smiled and kinda stared off into the distance for a while. What was that about?"

To which Daddy replied, "Oh, I knew your Uncle Corky was stacking the deck, but when you're the oldest, you will always look out for your younger brothers and sisters."

I smiled at Daddy and said, "Yes, sir, you're right."

**Lesson learned:** *Always remember, what goes in will come out. You'd better hope you're amongst friends that will tell you that you have a fly between your teeth.*

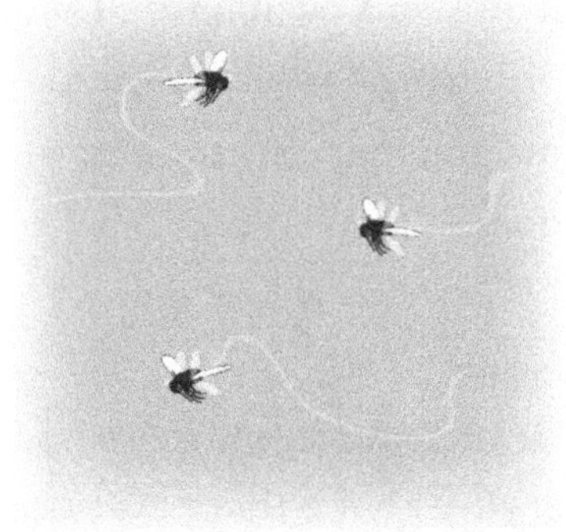

# Some days it's chickens, and some days it's feathers...

Guess I am airing out our dirty laundry here, but I will bet a dollar to a doughnut that I'm not the only one who grew up with some days being better than other days.

For this story, I am talking about money. That seems to be what the world uses to gauge good days by, isn't it? As young kids, a good life was if you got everything you had asked for when it came to your birthday or Christmas, or if after church every Sunday you went out to eat with family or the Pastor and his wife. That was a good life, right? Or where you went on summer vacation – that is, if you even got to go on a summer vacation.

There were those that went camping at the lake with their family in tents. Some got to go to summer horse-riding camps in other states, and then there were the elite kids who traveled abroad with their family. No matter the finances of their family, they got a summer vacation.

I truly believe this is an age thing for a child. We literally grow up happy and having fun, that is until someone tries to tell us our definition of having fun is not valid. If we did what they did, then that's fun. No, ma'am, that's their opinion. And my opinion counts just as much as theirs does.

For many years, my Daddy took care of Mother and us three kids earning $60.00 a week. No, that is not a typo. He worked Monday through Saturday for a whopping $60.00. You may say, yeah, but things were a lot cheaper back then, and you would be right.

As a matter of fact, I recently came across some old, cancelled checks Mother had kept, and the gas bill for their house was $1.67 back in the late 1950s. But then I say, put it down on paper. What all comes out of that $60.00 a week?

You have your tithe and offering for church, clothes, shoes, diapers, haircuts, school supplies, dentist bills, doctor bills, house rent, car payment, gas for the car, electric bill, telephone bill, house gas bill, car and life insurance, and food. When Daddy got paid on Saturday, the first thing he did was set aside his tithe and offerings for church the next morning.

I asked him one time why he gives the church money every Sunday, to which he replied, "Because you can't outgive God. In the Bible, it tells us our tithe is 10%, and we are expected to give that to the church we attend. We live off the remaining 90%."

"Why does the church need our money, Daddy?"

"Donna, God doesn't need our money, he needs our obedience. He teaches us to bring the tithes and offerings to the storehouse, which is the church. How do you think they pay the bills for the church doors to be open?"

"Oh," I said, "I never thought about it like that."

Daddy said, "I gladly give my tithe and offerings every Sunday, because you just can't outgive God. Any time there was a special need or want, I would pray, and without fail, God always provided."

And I, too, live by that today; you just can't outgive God. Aren't you glad God didn't say our tithe was 90%, and we could live on the remaining 10%? That's funny right there. Don't care who you are.

Most of the meat in our freezer was from fattening calves raised by Grandma and Papaw Gandee on their farm, and it tasted really good. We also had vegetables, along with jellies and jams, that had been canned and put either in the freezer or on the pantry shelves. When we were able to go to the drive-in movie theater (we couldn't afford the walk-in movie theaters), Mother would always make a big brown paper grocery bag of popcorn and a gallon of homemade sweet tea. We carried cups and took ice from the ice trays out of the icebox. And yes, that is what we called it – an icebox, not a refrigerator. We put the tea, along with the ice cubes, down in the ice chest, and off we would go. We were having fun and were as happy as a pig wallerin' in mud.

Funny how the world can dictate to us when we are rich or when we are poor, and it's all based on their opinion. I'm sitting here saying, hold up one cotton-picking minute. What about what I think?

When you have a roof over your head, clothes on your back, and food on the table, you are rich. That is the way I grew up viewing my life, because I saw so many who didn't even have that. It's true that "how you were raised" determines your viewpoint on happiness.

However, as I grew older, I started listening to some of the kids at school, and that's when some confusion set in. In case you hadn't noticed, kids can be cruel, especially to each other. My Grandma Gandee had sewn a lot of the clothes that I wore to school, and it was obvious they weren't "store-bought." They were made from print you didn't see at the nice dress stores nor at the fabric store. Most were what's called feed-sack material. Guess I had better explain myself.

Prior to the middle-1800s, flour, grain, wheat, and seeds were all packaged in barrels, boxes, or tins. Then, around the middle-to-late-1800s, cloth sacks or bags began replacing them. Don't want to bore you with a history lesson, but the history of feed sack material is definitely worth looking up. Suffice it to say, the feed sacks evolved when the manufacturers realized what the women were doing with them. And just like that, from necessity, a new fabric was born for those who couldn't afford the store-bought fabric of the day. Go to the feed store, pick up your supplies, and after you dump them in the bins, you had fabric to sew clothes with.

Most of the skirts and dresses that I wore were made from feed sack. Some were solid colors, and some were very pretty prints. All I knew was the material was pretty, and my grandma hand made it for me, fitting me to a T.

I wore those clothes with so much pride. But true to kids being kids, there came a time I started questioning things, like why I couldn't have more store-bought clothes like the other kids – the name-brand clothes, shoes, etc. Instead of talking about it with my parents, I decided I would talk to Grandma Gandee when I went to spend the weekend with her.

After eating a late lunch, we filled our tea glasses and went outside to sit by the honeysuckle on the east end of her garage. Oh, my gosh, that honeysuckle smelled so good! I figured this would be a good time to ask her for help.

I told her what the kids at school was telling me. She took a sip of her tea and asked me how that made me feel. To which I replied, "Grandma, I don't really know. They tell me I should feel bad, but somehow, I don't think I do."

She smiled and asked me why it didn't bother me. After sitting there for a few minutes, I gathered my thoughts.

"Well, Grandma, I have thought about it a lot, and I believe I have come to the conclusion that their lights are on, but no one's at home. Kids at school are basing their version of happiness on money and possessions. Nothing wrong with money or possessions, but those things are just that – things. I made a list of the things that are happy in my world. I live in a house, there's always food on the table, clean clothes to wear, and there's a family that loves me. I really think that everyone has their own opinion of what happiness is, and sometimes those opinions can be very different. So, Grandma, what do I tell them?"

She smiled and said, "Donna, that's a simple answer. Just tell them some days it's chickens, and some days it's feathers. What kind of day are you having?"

**Lesson learned:** *Not everyone will share your opinion, and how you respond will determine your happiness.*

# So, you think that's funny, do you?

Both Grandma Snow and Daddy has told me this story on more than one occasion. It was quite comical hearing her side of the story and then hearing his. While all the facts were the same, their take on the events of that day were different. And I have to admit, when I get a picture of this in my mind, I laugh all over again.

Now, there is about a three-year age difference between Daddy and his brother, my Uncle Corky. According to them, this story took place when Daddy was about 10 or 11, and Uncle Corky had to be around 7 going on 8.

Daddy and Uncle Corky were over at their Aunt Patsy Ruth's house on a Saturday, so that their mother, my Grandma Snow, could go shopping. Well, like most childhoods back then, kids mainly played outside. Aunt Patsy Ruth had all the windows in the house open, airing it out as she would say, while tending to her chores for the day. She had already put out, as she called it, "one load of laundry" on the clothesline to dry.

It just so happened that she was standing at the kitchen sink when she overheard her two nephews. Apparently, they were having a conversation that involved a few choice "cuss" words. Not thinking there was anyone within a hundred miles of them, Uncle Corky let fly a few four-letter words!

Aunt Patsy Ruth froze, thinking to herself, *Surely, I misunderstood what was said!*

So, she stopped what she was doing, stood very quietly, and continued to listen. And it only took a few moments before Uncle Corky let fly the same cuss words over and over again, both boys giggling in between each cuss word he let fly.

Now, hold this picture in your mind for a moment, and let me go off on a rabbit trail about Aunt Patsy Ruth.

Technically, she is my Great Aunt, but everyone called her Aunt Patsy Ruth. Let me make a general statement. I believe everyone has an "Aunt Patsy Ruth" in their family. She may have been the youngest of nine children, but let me tell you something. This woman ran a tight ship.

I grew up in a time where families got together for reunions, graduations, birthdays, wedding and baby showers, and celebrated "family." People actually knew who their first, second, and third cousins were. They spent the day together, eating home-cooked food, with menfolk sitting around playing cards and seeing who could tell the next big "fishing or hunting story." After the womenfolk finished tending to the food, they would all sit around talking themselves. Let me tell you, their conversations were quite interesting... and sometimes very colorful!

Aunt Patsy Ruth was what we all liked to call "the cruise director." Us kids were raised to respect and mind our elders, or suffer the consequences. Obviously, this included Aunt Patsy Ruth. Because the consequences of not minding her... Well, let's just say you definitely didn't want to go there. You not only got in trouble with her, but also when you got home, you were in trouble with your parents for embarrassing them at the family get-together.

Aunt Patsy Ruth kept all of us kids in line, and I am talking about at least 15 to 20 kids at a time. She was strict, but she was also fair. We all learned at an early age to not cross her, as she had a license to "whip legs." This Southern Baptist woman meant business.

Now, back to my original story. Aunt Patsy Ruth turned on her heels and headed for the back screen door off the kitchen, hollering with each step, "Hershel Lloyd, Harold Don!"

Side note – It doesn't matter how old you are. When someone, especially an elder, hollers your first and second name, it's not good. Not good at all.

Now, Daddy and Uncle Corky knew to answer her immediately. So, around the house, they were hollering, "Yes, ma'am we're coming!" as they ran up the back porch steps and into the house. They ran to see why Aunt Patsy Ruth was calling for them.

As they entered the kitchen, there she stood with her hands on her hips and *the look*. Oh, yes, you know what I am talking about when I say, "the look." The look on someone's face that is about to make your life flash before your eyes. The look that makes you freeze, because odds are your life, as you know it, is over.

While they knew by her body language that they were in trouble, they weren't exactly sure what it was for.

Aunt Patsy Ruth walked up to Uncle Corky and said, "So, you like saying cuss words, do you? Nasty, ugly words coming out of your mouth!"

With one hand, she took ahold of the top of his hair and tilted his head back. With the other hand, she pulled a bar of lye soap out of her apron pocket and jobbed it into his mouth, then pulled it out by raking it against the backside of his upper teeth. She was telling him the whole time, "We are gonna wash that filthy talk out of your mouth, young man!"

Well, evidently, it was quite a sight to see, so Daddy started laughing at Uncle Corky getting in trouble. She stepped back, and Uncle Corky is standing there crying and spitting bubbles. She turned to Daddy and said, "So, you think that's funny, do you?"

Then, she grabbed him by the top of the hair, tilted his head back, and did the same thing to him.

Daddy was hollering, crying, and through the bubbles managed to ask, "Aunt Patsy Ruth, I wasn't cussing. Why did I get in trouble?"

She stood back, looking at both her nephews, and replied, "That'll teach you to cuss, Hershel Lloyd, and that will teach you to laugh at your brother, Harold Don."

Both boys knew that if their mother found out they had gotten in trouble with Aunt Patsy Ruth, they would get it again when they got home. So, for the rest of the visit, they were perfect little angels. When their mother came to pick them up, as usual, she would ask, "Did the boys behave? Were they any trouble?"

Aunt Patsy Ruth looked at her nephews, grinned, turned back to her sister and said, "Nothing that a little lye soap and elbow grease didn't fix!"

**Lesson learned:** *If you wouldn't say it in front of Aunt Patsy Ruth, I suggest you don't say it at all. But if you're gonna take up cussing at an early age, be careful where you are standing. You never know who is listening.*

# Shiny and new doesn't always beat tried and true...

Many years, or should I say many decades ago, Daddy gave me my very first pocket watch. As of today, I have three pocket watches, but the value in this particular watch was because it was a gift from my Daddy.

It had several scratches on it, but that didn't matter to me. As Daddy pointed out, the case closed nice and tight, and it kept great time – "railroad time," as he would say. He had been told all his life that railroad time was the official time and what everyone went by. Well, I decided if it was good enough for my Daddy, it was good enough for me.

It did not come with a shiny gold chain like I had seen in the movies or any way to fasten it to the belt loop on my blue jeans. Then I realized, I carry keys in one pocket and loose change in the other.

I spoke up and said, "My pocket watch is gonna get all scratched up."

Daddy said, "Donna, just put it in the watch pocket on your blue jeans, and it won't get scratched."

I looked up at him and said, "Watch pocket?"

He laughed and said, "Hadn't you ever wondered what that little pocket is on the right side of your blue jeans?"

I said, "Wait a minute... What? That's what that little pocket is for?"

Daddy laughed and nodded his head. "Yes, ma'am, it is."

Evidently, what I was thinking in my head came out of my mouth when I said, "Wow, it is true. We can learn something new every day if we will just watch and listen."

Daddy looked at me and smiled.

"But don't I still need something to tie it off to my blue jeans with?" I asked.

"Yes, you do," Daddy said.

So, I just stood there, as lost as a goose in a snowstorm, waiting on him to tell me what to do. Daddy answered the confused look on my face by saying, "When you get to work tomorrow, go ask Uncle George for help."

He was talking about his uncle, so that would make him my Great Uncle George. Now, Uncle George was a craftsman just like his Daddy, my Great Grandpa Thoma. The menfolk in that family could repair anything, build anything, and fix any problem you had. Great Grandpa Thoma passed all his knowledge down to his sons and daughters, his grandsons, and his granddaughters.

Daddy said his Grandpa Thoma taught them how to build things, look at a problem, reason it out, and come up with a solution. He also taught him hunting, fishing, tracking, whittling, wood working, building houses, and the list goes on and on. I could tell by the way he spoke of his Grandpa how much he loved and respected him.

So, at the suggestion of my Daddy, I carried my pocket watch to work the next day and asked Uncle George for help.

He looked my watch over and said, "This is a mighty fine pocket watch, and you need a way to keep from losing it out of your blue jeans. Follow me."

So out to his work trailer we went. He rummaged around for a few minutes and came back with an old work boot, exclaiming, "This will work perfectly!"

Now, to be honest with you, my first thought was, *Surely, he had to be kidding with me*. But as it turned out, he wasn't kidding at all.

Now, in this old work trailer that held all his tools, he had a homemade table. He sat down at the table, placing my treasure on the table, and took out his pocketknife. Being very careful, he proceeded to cut off the upper leather part of this old work boot. Standing there in amazement, I just couldn't see how this old work boot had anything to do with my pocket watch.

Then my next thought was, *Why would anyone keep one old work boot with the sole worn off the bottom?*

As he looked over at me, I really think he was reading my mind. Uncle George spoke up and said, "You're probably wondering why I have kept a single work boot."

To which I answered him, "Yes, sir."

Setting his carpenter's pencil down, he sat up straight from leaning over the table and leaned back on his home-made stool. "There's a very good reason for that, Donna. Let me share something with you."

He started telling me a story about growing up and something his Daddy had told him.

"One thing we must always remember – use everything God has given us, and let nothing go to waste. Too many people throw things away that still have a value. Some throw friendships away, some throw educations away, some throw good jobs away, some throw their life away on drinking or drugs, and some even throw marriages away. Have you ever heard anyone say that one man's trash is another man's treasure?"

I responded, "Yes, sir, I have."

Uncle George smiled and said, "There is always a value if you will slow down long enough to look. Never forget that shiny and new doesn't always beat tried and true. My Daddy, your Great Grandpa, instilled that in each of us kids, and we in turn taught it to our kids with the hope that these life lessons will continue to be passed down from generation to generation."

He reached over his table, picking up the upper part of his work boot that he had cut off, and asked me what I saw.

My response was, "It's part of an old work boot."

"True, it is part of an old work boot, but it still has value. All comes down to your imagination as to what you could use it for. Let me explain about this work boot, Donna. The soles were worn down to literally almost nothing, non-repairable. However, the leather uppers were still in good shape. A can of grease was spilled on one of the boots, so now it was no longer useable. Would you have thrown both boots away, or just the ruined one?"

I didn't answer him.

"Work boots are usually made from really good sturdy leather, so I knew that the other boot still had value and would probably come in handy someday. And guess what? Today's that day. Keep watching and you will see the value appear right before your eyes."

With that, he picked up his carpenter's pencil, began carefully drawing on the leather, making sure everything was in proportion, and even using a ruler for his straight lines. Next, he pulled out a very sharp pocketknife and slowly cut out a strip of leather. With another tool, he put a hole in one end. He threaded the leather through the top piece of my pocket watch, ran the opposite end through the top part of the leather strip, and tightened it down. Then, with that half sideways grin on his face, he handed it to me and said, "Now you will never lose your watch."

I guarantee you, there is no gold chain on this earth that could ever compete with the handmade leather watch strap my Great Uncle George made for me. And thinking back on my life, I am proud to say that my Daddy did his job and passed on the "life lessons" his Grandpa taught him.

Uncle George is gone now, which makes it all the more valuable to me. I still have the watch and strap that was made for me from his old work boot.

**Lesson learned:** *Shiny and new doesn't always beat tried and true.*

# "What the wurld?"

Laney may only be three years old, but what an adventure these three years have been with her in my life.

Being around so many adults, her command of the English language began at an early age. Obviously, as with most kids, she would have a little trouble forming some of her words at first, not to mention putting words in the right context of a sentence.

Just like her mother, she's a cowgirl through and through. Even when asked what she wanted on her birthday cake, it was horses and bulls! There was, however, one very special horse in this story. Let me tell you about him.

As with all stories, it was love at first sight – a girl and her horse. She fell in love with one of my retired rope horses, Sammy. From the very moment she laid eyes on him, she started telling everyone that Sammy was "her horse."

Now, Sammy is a big bay horse, 31 years old now, and stands over 16.3 hands tall. He is a big boy. To be honest with you, I think Sammy fell in love with her too. I believe in my heart that Sammy knew they belonged together.

Every morning and every evening, after putting on her pink mud boots, Laney would go to the feed room, get her bucket of feed, put it in the wagon she pulled behind her little John Deere tractor, drive down to the hay barn, and get a flake of hay. Then, she'd drive across the yard over to the pasture where Sammy was. Her mother would help by lifting her up to put the feed in his bucket. While he would eat, Laney would stand and pet on him and hug his legs. That was about all she could reach.

This gentle giant knew she was there, being very careful not to step on her. You could tell he thoroughly enjoyed his feed and the love of this little girl. Oh, what a pair they became. Her mother would put a halter on him, set Laney up on his back, and lead them around. Laney was in what we call "hog heaven," loving every minute she spent with her horse.

I think one of the cutest things was to watch her brush him. Since he was so tall, and she was so short, she could only reach his legs and the bottom of his belly. Ha!

Well, now that you have a little background on Laney and her horse Sammy, let me tell you what happened.

Several of us were sitting around one evening, discussing a recent rodeo, particularly the barrel racing event. Laney walked into the room and began listening to our conversation. Out of nowhere, Laney decided she needed to interrupt our conversation, as she had something to contribute. She proceeded to tell us that she and Sammy ran barewuls (barrels) at that same rodeo.

We all stopped our adult conversation, and our attention turned to Laney. Looking over at her grandmother standing next to me, under my breath, I said, "This ought to be good."

I looked down and asked her, "You were at the rodeo today and ran barrels?"

Laney nodded yes. Not letting this chance pass me by, as I could not wait to hear the answer, I asked her, "How did she do? Did you win?"

And thus began Laney's version of her running barrels on Sammy.

"I was running barewuls on Sammy at the rodeo. I went around the first barewul, and then I fell off!"

With my hands up in the air and a surprised look on my face, I immediately said to Laney, "Oh, my gosh, were you hurt?"

She said no and that Sammy just stopped and looked at her. Since I knew she has a very vivid imagination, I asked her, "What did Sammy do?"

She set her baby doll down on the floor and proceeded to put both her little hands up in the air, slightly bent over, and said, "Sammy looked at me and said, 'What the wurld?'" (Meaning, "What the world?")

Trying my best to keep a straight face, I asked her what happened then.

She said, "Well, I looked at Sammy and said, 'Oh, balls,' then got back on him, and we won the barewul race."

At the end of her story, she picked up her baby doll and walked out of the kitchen. This child was being as serious as she could be telling her story, so you can imagine how hard it was not to laugh. But we did manage to hold it in until she was out of the room.

We all knew where "What the world?" came from, as she was trying to say, "What in the world?" But where did "Oh, balls" come from? Didn't take long to figure out it was from her grandfather.

Well, Laney's mother told her dad, "When she starts school and I get that first phone call about 'oh, balls,' I am referring them to you!"

**Lesson learned:** *Be careful what you say, how you say it, and who you say it in front of. Out of the mouths of babes!*

# Carl, Carl, Carl...

There are many things I remember about my life growing up, and one of them is the subject of this story.

It revolves around Grandma and Papaw Snow, and I can still hear her hollering at him, "Carl, Carl, Carl!"

This was the beginning of every sentence when she was mad, and on the end of her sentence would be the reason for her being upset with him. Nine times out of ten, it was because he was saying or doing something in front of us grandkids that she didn't approve of and evidently thought the only way to get his attention to relay her dislike was by hollering his name three times.

It was never once, nor twice, but always three times. Never figured that one out. Things that make you go, *Hmmm.* Although, I do admit, her method of operation always seemed to work, as it always got his attention.

To the best of my recollection, Papaw seemed to stay in a lot of trouble with Grandma. I am the oldest of eight grandchildren, and therefore I heard and saw a lot of things my cousins didn't. Some things made me giggle, and some things made me sad.

One of the things I can distinctly remember was a story that Grandma Snow told me surrounding events when I was around 1-2 years old.

Like I said, I am the oldest grandchild of eight. When I was born, it was 8:29 p.m., which meant this was an all-day affair. As you can imagine, all grandparents and soon-to-be aunts and uncles were present. Back in this time period, there wasn't anything like sonograms, so there was no way to know if this bouncing bundle of joy was a boy or a girl.

It seems that everyone was hoping I was a boy. Well, guess what? I wasn't. In fact, Daddy was thoroughly convinced I would be a boy. Grandma Snow told me she asked him why he thought this, and he replied, "Mother, you had a boy first, so shouldn't I have a boy first?"

I told her, "Sounds like Daddy didn't pay close attention in health or science class, did he?"

The doctor came out and said, "Harold, you are the proud Daddy of a baby girl, with ten fingers and ten toes. Mother and daughter are doing fine." And that was about the extent of information given out at that time.

Grandma Snow told me after she talked to Daddy, he was okay with me being a girl and not a boy.

"How do you know he was telling you the truth, Grandma?"

"Well, he didn't try to send you back to the factory now, did he?"

I have to admit, she caught me off guard with that one.

It seems that Papaw Snow had his mind made up that he was going to give this first grandchild, me, a nickname like he did Uncle Corky. Evidently, he hadn't shared this idea with anyone else. To be honest with you, I think the man was building up his courage to tell Grandma Snow what he intended to do.

While Grandma Snow was a short lady, she was the very description of dynamite in a small package. You mess with any of her kids or grandkids, you should just as soon go bear hunting with a switch.

Well, the day came, and he must have felt this would be the best time to let her know of his plans. Grandma said he came home from work one day and made his announcement. He had decided to give me a nickname, and the nickname was "Spooky."

Grandma said she looked at him like he had done gone and lost his mind. As a matter of fact, she asked him if he had indeed lost his mind. "Where on God's green earth did you come up with a nickname like that?"

To which he replied, "That's my one of my favorite comic strip characters."

To which Grandma replied, "Carl, Carl, Carl! There is no way I am letting you call this baby Spooky. She's a sweet little girl and not a rough little boy. And I think the only one who would be happy with the nickname would be you."

It's my understanding that this caused, let's say, a little riff between them. Or you could call it a small debate. Or you could call it what it actually was.

Grandma was so bent out of shape that she stopped speaking to him. While Grandma thought she was making him suffer, others told me Papaw didn't mind at all. He was kinda glad she stopped chewing him out.

So, once the obligatory "be mad at each other" time passed, he tried again. And again, he went down in flames. So, being the resourceful man that he was, he went out and bought a house-moving pull truck, a 1955 Model White, gasoline engine, and named it Spooky.

He even had the name painted on the side of the truck. In an effort to get the last word in, which can prove difficult with any woman, Daddy told me my Papaw Snow had him stand me up in the driver's side of the truck and took my picture.

When the dust settled, to some degree, I would have to say that Papaw Snow got his way, Grandma Snow got her way, and all was right in their world once again. That is, until the next time he heard, "Carl, Carl, Carl..."

**Lesson learned:** *When your wife calls you by your name three times, that's not a good sign.*

# About the Author

Donna Snow King is a proud, multi-generational Texan, born and raised in Fort Worth. Growing up a third generation house mover, which started with her Grandpa Snow in 1942, eventually led her to the TV world where she and her sister, Toni, (The Snow Sisters) were introduced to the world.

H.D. Snow and Son House Moving, Inc. has been a huge part of her life with her Daddy, H.D. Snow, her brother, and her sister. During her off time from moving houses and historical buildings, she volunteers not only at her church but also mentoring youth at the local high school rodeo associations, as well as an advocate for our Military, Veterans, and their families. Donna is happily married to the love of her life, Rex. They are enjoying life on the Snow King Ranch. With both Donna and her husband holding Amateur Radio Licenses, you can often hear them on their Ham Radios. Their call signs are W5SML and W5EAK. Her philosophy in life is to never miss a good chance to sow a seed by helping someone.

Printed in the USA
CPSIA information can be obtained
at www.ICGtesting.com
LVHW011210061223
765454LV00073B/1928